100 ANIMAL COOKIES

100 ANIMAL COOKIES

A Super-Cute Menagerie to Decorate Step-by-Step

Lisa Snyder

A QUINTET BOOK

First published in the UK in 2014 by Apple Press
74-77 White Lion Street,
London N1 9PF
United Kingdom

www.apple-press.com

ISBN: 978-1-84543-564-6

QTT.ANIC

Conceived, designed, and produced by
Quintet Publishing Limited
114-116 Western Road
Hove, East Sussex
BN3 1DD
United Kingdom

Designer: Astwood Design
Photographer: Tony Briscoe
Art Director: Michael Charles
Editorial Director: Emma Bastow
Publisher: Mark Searle
Editorial Assistant: Ella Lines

Printed in China by 1010 Printing International Limited

9 8 7 6 5 4 3 2 1

Contents

Introduction

When I was a little girl, I would spend days with my grandmother just so I could play in the kitchen while she cooked. Her banana pudding and chocolate tart were out of this world! I was eager to learn, so she would pull a chair over to the kitchen worktop and give me a banana and a butter knife so I could cut the bananas. Helping her prepare her special banana pudding made me feel like a grown-up even though I was only six years old.

I believe my passion for baking was born as I stood on that kitchen chair watching and working alongside one of my favourite people in the world. Since then I have always enjoyed baking for my friends and family, but it was not until sometime later that I discovered a direction for my baking passion.

One day, while cleaning the house, I watched Martha Stewart on television. She had a cookie artist named Dani Fiori on the show that day. Dani made the cutest decorated cookies I had ever seen – one cookie not only caught my eye but stole my heart: a Father Christmas cookie made from Martha Stewart's Holiday Cookie Cutter Collection. I knew I had to have that cookie cutter.

Macy's was the only shop that sold that specific Father Christmas cookie cutter, but they were already sold out. I quickly grabbed my computer and started searching until I found the Father Christmas cutter on an auction site. I placed a bid and waited and watched as someone bid against me. It was a battle of wills and I am happy, and embarrassed, to say that I won. Yikes! Did I really pay £35 for a cookie cutter!? Yes I did.

I paid way too much for that little Father Christmas cutter but every time I make cookies with that cutter, I am reminded of how much I loved baking with my grandmother. I guess it was worth every penny.

Soon after getting my hands on that special cookie cutter, I began to experiment with icing, other cookie cutters, and every technique I could think of to make my cookies stand out. I was excited about the things I discovered and I wanted to share my new-found techniques with anyone who would listen (or read). Hence my blog – *The Bearfoot Baker* (*www.thebearfootbaker.com*) – was born.

The Bearfoot Baker is a way for me to share my love of cutout cookies and teach others how to become cookie artists. You do not have to have fancy equipment, and you definitely do not need to pay £35 for a single cookie cutter. You just need to know a few simple steps and techniques.

I hope you find some inspiration in *100 Animal Cookies*. If the tips and tricks I offer here open a world of cookie decorating for you, I encourage you to share a little sweetness with others, just as my grandmother and Dani Fiori did with me.

Lisa Snyder

Basic Cookie Recipes

The base for any cutout cookie is a simple flavoured, baked cookie dough. I have three basic but delicious cookie dough recipes that I use frequently, and they all work well with royal icing and the other decorations called for in this book. Choose your favourite, switch it up based on the season, or just mix and match as desired.

Vanilla Cookies

SUPPLIES

- ◆ 600g (1lb 5oz) plain flour
- ◆ ½ teaspoon baking powder
- ◆ ½ teaspoon salt
- ◆ 225g (8oz) unsalted butter, softened
- ◆ 340g (12oz) granulated sugar
- ◆ 120g (4oz) icing sugar
- ◆ 2 eggs
- ◆ 1 teaspoon vanilla extract
- ◆ 1 teaspoon almond extract

1. Mix the flour, baking powder, and salt together in a bowl and set aside.

2. Cream the butter, granulated sugar, and icing sugar together using a handheld electric whisk or a freestanding mixer. Whisk until pale and fluffy. Add the eggs, vanilla and almond extracts and mix until fully combined.

3. Add the flour mixture to the butter mixture two tablespoonfuls at a time, mixing after each addition, until fully incorporated. Scrape the bottom and sides of the bowl between additions to be sure all ingredients are evenly incorporated.

4. Divide the dough into three and wrap each third in cling film. Chill the wrapped dough for at least an hour. Note: Frozen dough has a tendency to spread, but chilled dough does not. In order for your cutout cookies to hold their intended shape, it is best to start with chilled but not frozen dough.

5. When you are ready to shape your cookies, preheat the oven to 180ºC/350ºF/gas mark 4.

6. Roll out the chilled dough until it is 1cm (½in) thick on a cutting mat. Cover the rolled dough with cling film and place the dough and the mat into the freezer for about 15 minutes.

7. Turn the mat upside-down onto a clean surface and carefully peal the mat away from the dough (this will prevent your cut cookie shapes from sticking to the mat). Place the dough back onto the mat and remove the cling film.

8. Line a baking sheet with baking parchment. Cut the cookie shapes with your chosen cookie cutter and transfer the cookie shapes to the lined baking sheet. The cookie shapes should stick inside the cutter as you lift it from the mat – simply set the cutter with dough inside onto the baking sheet, and gently press the dough out without altering the shape of the cookie.

9. Bake for 8 to 10 minutes, or until the edges begin to brown. Allow the cookies to cool on the baking sheet for 15 minutes, then transfer to a wire rack to cool completely.

Makes approximately 30 cookies, depending on the size of your cutter.

TIPS & TRICKS

If the cookies are not coming out right for you, try them at a higher temperature. In one of my ovens they bake better at 190ºC/375ºF/gas mark 5 for the same length of time.

Chocolate Cookies

SUPPLIES

- ◆ 110g (3½oz) unsalted butter, softened
- ◆ 110g (3½oz) white vegetable fat
- ◆ 225g (8oz) granulated sugar
- ◆ 1 egg
- ◆ 1 teaspoon vanilla extract
- ◆ 1 teaspoon strong brewed coffee
- ◆ ½ teaspoon salt
- ◆ 110g (3½oz) cocoa powder
- ◆ 375g (13oz) plain flour

1. Mix the butter and shortening together using a handheld electric whisk or a free-standing mixer on a low setting. Scrape the sides of the bowl and mix again.

2. Add the sugar and whisk to combine. Add the egg, vanilla extract and coffee and whisk again.

3. Add the salt and cocoa and whisk on a low setting until well combined – scrape the bottom and sides of the bowl often to ensure all ingredients are evenly incorporated.

4. Add the flour, two tablespoonfuls at a time, mixing after each addition, until fully incorporated.

5. Divide the dough into three and wrap each third in cling film. Chill for at least an hour. Note: Frozen dough has a tendency to spread, but chilled dough does not. In order for your cutout cookies to hold their intended shape, it is best to start with chilled but not frozen dough.

6. When you are ready to shape your cookies, preheat the oven to 180ºC/350ºF/gas mark 4. Follow the instructions for the vanilla cookies on page 7, adjusting the cooking time to 9 to 11 minutes.

Gingerbread Cookies

SUPPLIES

- ◆ 900g (2lb) plain flour
- ◆ ¼ teaspoon salt
- ◆ ½ teaspoon bicarbonate of soda
- ◆ 1 tablespoon ground ginger
- ◆ 1½ teaspoons ground cloves
- ◆ 2 teaspoons ground cinnamon
- ◆ 1 teaspoon ground nutmeg
- ◆ 225g (8oz) unsalted butter, softened
- ◆ 175g (6oz) light soft brown sugar
- ◆ 2 eggs
- ◆ 250g (9oz) black treacle
- ◆ 2 teaspoons vanilla extract

1. In a bowl, mix together the flour, salt, bicarbonate of soda, ginger, cloves, cinnamon, and nutmeg. Set aside.

2. Cream the butter and sugar together using a handheld electric whisk or a freestanding mixer until pale and creamy. Add the eggs one at a time, beating well after each addition. Add the treacle and vanilla extract and mix to combine.

3. Add the flour mixture to the butter mixture two tablespoonfuls at a time, mixing after each addition, until fully incorporated. Scrape the bottom and sides of the bowl between additions to be sure all ingredients are evenly incorporated.

4. Divide the dough into three and wrap each third in cling film. Chill for at least an hour. Note: Frozen dough has a tendency to spread, but chilled dough does not. In order for your cutout cookies to hold their intended shape, it is best to start with chilled but not frozen dough.

5. When you are ready to shape your cookies, preheat the oven to 180ºC/350ºF/gas mark 4. Follow instructions for the vanilla cookies on page 7, adjusting the cooking time to 6 to 8 minutes.

Royal Icing

Royal icing is a cookie artist's paint and I use it, in one form or another, in every recipe in this book. This simple royal icing recipe uses meringue powder and icing sugar. It is perfect for decorating cutout cookies because it dries with a smooth, hard surface, and it is easy to tint with soft gel colouring pastes that will not water down your icing.

SUPPLIES

- ◆ 1.125kg (2¼lb) icing sugar
- ◆ 180ml (6fl oz) water
- ◆ 5 tablespoons meringue powder
- ◆ 1 teaspoon cream of tartar (omit this ingredient if it is already included in your brand of meringue powder)
- ◆ 1 teaspoon vanilla extract

1. Measure the icing sugar into the bowl of a freestanding mixer. (You can use a handheld electric whisk, but this icing is very stiff and may damage your machine. Add a little water to thin the icing if necessary.) Stir with a whisk to remove any lumps and set aside.

2. Whisk the water, meringue powder, cream of tartar (if using) and vanilla together in a measuring jug or bowl, then add to the icing sugar.

3. Using the paddle attachment with the mixer on a low setting, combine the wet ingredients with the sugar. Mix until all of the icing sugar is wet, then increase the speed to medium/high and continue mixing for about 1 minute.

4. Place the icing in an airtight container. Before covering the container with the lid, cover the top of the icing with cling film, pressing gently to completely cover the top of the icing. Air will cause the icing to form a crust, so make sure the cling film is touching the icing before you add the lid. Store the icing this way until you are ready to decorate the cookies. For tips and techniques on tinting and colouring icing and adjusting icing consistency, see page 13.

TIPS & TRICKS

There are two ways to make royal icing. One is with raw egg whites and the other is with meringue powder. I prefer to use meringue powder so I do not have to worry about the health risks that may be associated with eating raw eggs. Meringue powder is a fine white powder made mostly from dried egg whites. Most manufacturers also add cornflour to prevent it forming lumps. When it is added to water and mixed with icing sugar, it becomes a white royal icing. You can find meringue powder at cake supply shops and in craft shops. It is also available online.

Tools and Equipment

Simple iced cutout cookies can be made using equipment you probably already have in your kitchen. As your skills progress, you may want to invest in a few specialist tools – here are my suggestions.

AIRBRUSH GUN An airbrush gun is an easy way to add shadow and character to your cookies. To airbrush cookies, you will need to use special airbrush colours (do not use regular food colour or gel in an airbrush gun). For complete instructions on how to use an airbrush gun, see page 14.

COOKIE CUTTERS There are many different types of cookie cutters you can purchase. Copper cutters will last forever but cost more than tin and plastic cutters. I am not picky about the type of cutter I use – I like them all. As long as the cutter is made from a food safe material and has a cute shape, I will add it to my collection. If you cannot find a cookie cutter shape you want, you can hand cut the dough with a sharp knife.

COUPLERS Plastic couplers are used with piping bags. The coupler has two parts. One is referred to as the base and the other is the ring. The base fits narrow end first into a piping bag that has had the tip cut off. A decorating nozzle fits onto the base and is secured in place with a ring.

DISPOSABLE PIPING BAGS Because these disposable bags are very soft sided, they allow you to apply as much or as little pressure as you need and remain in full control of how much icing comes from the tip. While these are considered disposable, you can wash and dry them and use them multiple times. To use them, place the coupler into the bag, narrow end first. Push it down as far as it will go. Mark the spot on the outside of the bag at the first thread of the coupler that is closest to the end. Remove the coupler base and snip the bag at the mark you made. Insert the coupler base back into the bag. Place a decorating nozzle over the coupler and end of the bag. Secure by screwing on the ring.

EDIBLE PEARLS Edible pearls are great for making royal icing eyes. Add them to wet royal icing and allow them to dry in place.

They come in different sizes and colours. I most commonly use 4mm black edible pearls for eyes, but I also use larger black pearls for noses and white ones for decoration.

FAN When royal icing dries, it may end up with a very dull finish. If you want your icing to dry with a bit of a shine, place the cookies in front of a fan while they are drying. The air from the fan will give your cookies a nice shiny finish.

ICING SMOOTHER Use this tool to gently glide over the top of your base cookies as soon as you take them out of the oven. This will smooth out any bubbles and make the top of the cookie flat for easy decorating.

FOOD-COLOUR PENS There are a wide variety of food-colour pens on the market. I have tried almost all of them and I prefer AmeriColor and FooDoodlers. Experiment until you find a brand you like.

GEL PASTE COLOURS Soft gel paste colours work best for colouring and tinting royal icing. Regular food colouring can thin your icing and affect your ability to pipe. See page 13 for more on colouring royal icing.

ICING BAG TIES OR RUBBER BANDS It is helpful to wrap a bag tie around the top of a filled disposable decorating bag to prevent the icing oozing out of the top, and to stop the icing from drying out. Wilton (see Suppliers on page 144) makes bag ties for this purpose, or you can use rubber bands.

FOOD COLOUR DUST A flavourless powder, food colour dust comes in a wide variety of colours and is a great way to add a little colour to animal cookie cheeks and ears. It can be used on royal icing, sugarpaste and gum paste. It is best applied with a dry, soft, food-safe paintbrush.

PIPING NOZZLES These small metal cones are shaped to make different icing designs when the icing is pushed through them. The nozzle openings come in different shapes and sizes. Popular brands include Wilton, Tala and PME. Almost all of the cookies in this book were decorated with a No. 2 nozzle unless otherwise instructed. The No. 2 nozzle is a plain nozzle and is great for outlining and flooding.

ROLLING PIN A rolling pin is a must-have tool when making cookies. There are many types to choose from. I prefer a wooden rolling dowel that is a single thickness for its full length and does not taper at the ends. The dowel, along with the use of rolling pin spacers (see below), allows you to roll a wide piece of dough without cutting into the edges of the dough. If you use a rolling pin that tapers, the spacers need to be placed at the widest place on the rolling pin, which is often an area that is a lot narrower than your dough.

ROLLING PIN SPACERS Spacers can be placed on the ends of a rolling pin to ensure that you roll the cookie dough evenly before baking. I use the 1cm (½in) spacers for all my cookies.

ROYAL ICING TRANSFERS These prepared, dried shapes made with royal icing look great and are a real time-saver for a cookie decorator. For complete instructions on how to make royal icing transfers, see pages 15–17.

SPRINKLES AND SANDING SUGAR Sprinkles and sanding sugar are a great way to add texture and colour to an iced cookie. All you have to do is sprinkle it onto wet icing, wait a few seconds and shake off the excess. See page 14 for instructions on making your own sprinkles with royal icing.

SQUEEZE BOTTLES These plastic bottles come in a few different sizes. I prefer the 50g (2oz) and 225g (8oz) bottles, both used with a coupler. These bottles allow you to change the size of the decorating nozzle and are great for flooding cookies.

COCKTAIL STICK OR SKEWER Use a cocktail stick or skewer to help push icing into corners that the piping nozzle will not reach. You can also use it to pop any air bubbles in the flooded icing.

TWEEZERS Food safe tweezers are handy for adding pearls, beads and royal icing transfers to cookies.

Techniques

Creating beautiful animal cookies is easy when you know how. Once you've mastered these simple techniques, you will be baking and icing to your heart's content.

COMBINING COOKIE CUTTERS Sometimes it is hard to find a cookie cutter that works for a design you have in mind. It is very simple to combine two or three cutters to create a shape that will work for your needs. Learning this technique opens a whole new world for cookie decorators.

Begin by sketching a basic pattern for the animal you want to make. Look at the pattern with an open mind and think about which cutters will work. Think of the cutters like puzzle pieces that you can fit together to create new shapes – some shapes can overlap to make the fit just right.

Once you have chosen which cutters to combine, use them to cut the shapes out of raw dough and assemble them on a baking sheet. Use your fingers to gently press the cookies together but be careful not to alter their shape. As the cookies bake they will merge together, and once baked it will be as if you are working with one cookie.

Cookies that are pieced together do have a greater chance of breaking than a cookie that came from a solid shape. Here are a few tips to help prevent breakage:

• Try to combine shapes that fit together well. If you can embed one cookie piece into another, there will be less chance of breakage.

• Do not move the cookies from the baking sheet until they are completely cool. If you try to move the cookies when they are warm, you will weaken the seam and they will be at more risk of breakage.

• When decorating combination cookies, cover the seams with icing. The icing will help to hold the pieces together.

The Beaver base cookie on page 65 is made by combining star, frog and squirrel cookie cutters.

PREPARING AND FILLING A PIPING BAG Prepare the piping bag by unscrewing the coupler and placing the large part, thread-end down, inside the bag. Put it as far as you can towards the tip of the bag. Use scissors to score the bag just below the coupler. Remove the coupler and cut the bag at the scored line. Insert the coupler back into the bag. Place a piping nozzle on the bag and coupler and screw on the cap.

To fill the bag with icing, hold the bag and cuff the top over your hand. Use a spoon to scoop and push the icing down towards the tip of the bag as far as you can. Fill the bag a little over half way with

icing. Unfold the top of the bag. With your hands, gently squeeze the sides of the icing to push the air and air bubbles to the top. Twist the top of the bag and wrap with an icing bag tie or rubber band.

OUTLINING AND FLOODING Outlining and flooding are icing application techniques. Outlining a cookie refers to piping a line of icing that will act as a border or dam to hold the icing in place. Flooding a cookie is the act of filling an area (within the outlines) with icing. Without an outline, your icing can fall off the edge of the cookie. You can also pipe an outline in the centre of a cookie to keep colours from running into each other. If you think of the cookie

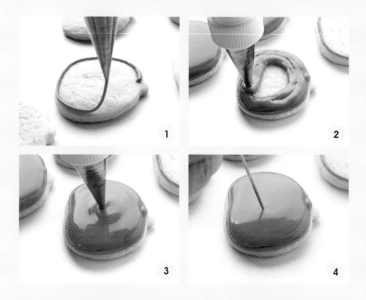

as a colouring book page, the outline will make the pattern on the cookie so you can later colour it in (flood) with icing.

To outline a cookie, place the tip of the icing bag close to the cookie and squeeze gently until the royal icing comes out of the tip. Then, let the icing touch the cookie and begin to lift the tip away from the cookie while continuing to add gentle pressure. Work your way around the edge of the cookie until you have a full outline (1). Once the outline is complete, start to flood the inside of the cookie by working around the outline (2). Keep flooding the cookie by going around the cookie until you reach the centre and then gently lift the piping bag away (3). Once your cookie is completely flooded, gently shake and tap the cookie on the work surface to help the icing flatten out. Use a cocktail stick to pop any air bubbles (4).

COLOURING ROYAL ICING
To mix royal icing colours, place some royal icing in a bowl – whatever amount you need in a single colour – and add a few drops of soft gel paste food colour. Mix, adding more gel paste if necessary, until the icing reaches the desired shade. Because it only takes a few drops to colour the icing, the addition of gel will not affect the consistency of the icing. Soft gel paste comes in a wide variety of colours, but you will sometimes still want to mix colours to get the right shade.

Soft gel pastes are sold in bakery supply shops, craft shops, online cookie supply shops, and in the craft sections of some department shops. The most common brands are Wilton and AmeriColor. Wilton pastes are sold in 25g (1oz) jars, and AmeriColor in 20g (¾oz), 175g

(6oz) and 390g (13½oz) bottles. To add Wilton colours to your icing, use a cocktail stick to add a small amount of the gel to the icing. It does not take much to tint the icing, so add a little at a time until you achieve the desired colour. AmeriColor has squeeze top bottles that allow you to squeeze one drop at a time into the icing. It is a convenient way to add the gel to the icing without a cocktail stick.

Most food colour gels do not have a flavour, but there are a few colours that have a bitter taste. Black, red, pink and purple are the ones I mix a little differently to avoid bitterness.

• To make black icing, try mixing brown and green pastes together to make a deep tint base and then add a few drops of black gel. The less black gel paste you use, the less bitter the taste.

• Red and pink food colour gels also have a bitter taste. Try Wilton No Taste Red. Or if you prefer AmeriColor, try using the Tulip Red. They are great colours and make a beautiful red or pink icing without the bitter taste.

• Purple gel paste can be strong and have a bitter taste. If you want purple icing without the bitter flavour, make your own purple icing by mixing Wilton No Taste Red or AmeriColor Tulip Red with blue gel.

• Adding pure vanilla extract to royal icing improves the taste, but it can turn the icing an off white or ivory colour. If you are colouring the icing, you probably will not notice the off white colour, but if you want white icing, you can add a small amount of bright white gel paste to make the icing pure white.

ROYAL ICING CONSISTENCY
Once you have achieved the desired colour, you need to make the icing the right consistency for decorating. All of the cookies in this book are decorated using my 15 second royal icing, unless otherwise stated. The '15 seconds' refers to when the tip of a knife is pulled through the icing, it will take 15 seconds for the line in the icing to disappear.

The other icing consistency used in my designs is referred to as 'thick' royal icing. Thick icing is thick enough to hold a shape. If you make a zigzag line with a star nozzle and thick icing, it will hold that shape and not flatten out. It is used to make the fur on the Penguin hats (see page 94) and the wings of the Swan cookies (see page 28).

To change the consistency of royal icing, add water one drop at a time and mix well after each addition. Pull a knife through the top of the icing and count how many seconds it takes for the line to disappear. Add a little more water if needed. If the line disappears before the 15 seconds are up, you may need to add a little icing sugar to make it thicker.

WET-ON-WET Wet-on-wet is a term used for piping wet icing onto wet icing. This method can be used to make the colours flow into each other by pulling a cocktail stick through the icing colours before they dry.

PAINTING ON A COOKIE The great thing about painting designs onto a cookie is that you only need one colour of icing. The details can then be painted onto this base colour. Also, I have never had a painted cookie bleed, as the gel colour stays where it is painted.

The cookies in this book were painted with a 10/0 food safe paintbrush. You can use any detail brush you are comfortable with, but this is my brush of choice. To paint on a cookie, dip the tip of your brush into a small amount of water. Then, dip the brush into a very small amount of food colour gel and paint a few lines on a plate or piece of baking parchment to blend the gel and water together. Paint the colour onto the cookie using gentle strokes, pulling the brush towards you. Repeat until the area is covered.

ROYAL ICING DRYING TIME To give your design definition, flood different sections of the cookie one at a time and wait for about 20 minutes before flooding the section beside it. This delay between floods will help to keep the sections defined. For example, the eyes on the Puffer Fish cookie on page 107 look like two eyes instead of one big eye with two black dots.

If instructions call for letting a cookie dry overnight, it is usually because there is a risk of the colours bleeding together. Sometimes it is best to be patient and allow the icing to completely dry before moving on to the next step so your cookie decorations will remain sharp, as intended.

AIRBRUSHING Airbrushing is a fast way to add shading and detail to a cookie. Refer to your owner's manual to set up your machine. To airbrush cookies, you will need to use special airbrush colours for an airbrush machine. You cannot use regular food colour or gel in your machine.

Begin by covering your work surface with baking parchment to prevent any unwanted spray from getting on your counter. This will also make cleaning up a breeze. Cover any area of the cookie you do not want sprayed with a kitchen towel or cling film. You will need to weigh the covering down with something so the air from the gun does not blow it away.

Add a drop or two of airbrush colour in the cup of the gun and turn on your machine. Spray a test spot on a kitchen towel or baking parchment before you begin to decorate the cookie.

Hold the tip of the airbrush gun about 3.5cm (1½in) away from the cookie and apply gentle pressure to the trigger. Move the airbrush gun constantly when pulling the trigger or you will get a messy spot on the cookie. The closer you hold the gun to the cookie the thinner the spray line will be. If you want a detail line, hold the gun close to the cookie. If you want to spray a mist on a large area, hold the gun several inches away from the cookie. Work your way around the cookie or area you want sprayed. Leave it to dry for a few minutes.

Airbrushing with a stencil is a great way to add a pretty pattern to a cookie. Place the stencil on a decorated cookie. Hold the stencil in place and gently spray with the colour of your choice. I usually spray the cookie with a colour that is a shade darker than my icing colour.

PETAL DUST APPLICATION Petal dust is a great way to add a little colour to animal cookie cheeks and ears and it is very easy to apply. Begin with a dry decorated cookie. Dip the tip of a dry food safe brush into the food colour dust. Tap the brush on the side of the container to shake off some dust. Gently rub the brush in a circular motion until you get the colour you desire. Gently shake off the excess dust or hold the cookie upside down and tap the back to remove any unwanted dust.

DIY SPRINKLES You can make custom sprinkles to match any icing colour by piping some lines with a No. 2 plain round nozzle onto a piece of wax paper or baking parchment and allowing them to dry completely. Once they are dry, break them into small pieces. You can store them in an airtight container in a dry place away from the sun. They will last for several months.

STAND-UP COOKIES Stand-up cookies make great centrepieces or place cards for a table and they are easy to make. With a few adjustments, almost any cookie can become a standing cookie. To make an animal cookie stand, you will need a base cookie and you will need to trim the bottom of the cookie you want to stand with a sharp knife before you bake it.

During the baking process, the cookie may spread a little and that will affect the standing ability of the cookie. No worries, just shave the bottom of the cookie with a food grater. Be careful not to shave the cookie at an angle. If angled, the cookie will not stand up straight.

Once the cookies are baked and trimmed, decorate both cookies and let them dry completely. To assemble the cookies, place a small amount of icing on the bottom of the cookie that you want to stand up. Place it in position on the base cookie and support it with two baking racks or other stacked cookies to let it dry overnight.

Royal Icing Transfers

A royal icing transfer is royal icing that has been piped onto wax paper, dried, and peeled off the wax paper to save for later use. They are simply made using a pattern, icing, wax paper, tape, and a flat surface.

Royal icing transfers are one of my favourite decorating tools. I live in a humid area and humidity causes royal icing colours to bleed into each other. Royal icing transfers really help to prevent the bleeding of icing colours, plus the transfers can be made in advance to save time on decorating. I have a lot of different transfer patterns on my blog so be sure to check often for new patterns you can use.

HOW TO MAKE ROYAL ICING TRANSFERS

1. Trace or print the template to use for your transfers. Place the template on a flat surface, such as a cutting board, and secure in place with masking or painter's tape.

2. Cover the template with a piece of wax paper and tape that down, too, making sure there are no wrinkles.

3. Pipe the pattern onto the wax paper using the template beneath as a guide. Allow the icing to dry completely – this may take a couple of days depending on the humidity in your area.

4. Gently remove the royal icing transfers from the wax paper and store them in airtight containers away from the sun. If you are trying to remove a delicate transfer, using a sharp edge, such as the edge of a bench scraper, will help to remove it in one piece.

I have jars full of different sized eyes and noses to use on my cookies. Once the cookie base coat is flooded, I just put the royal icing transfers in place and move on to the next step. You can make teeth, beaks, eyes, noses, acorns, bows or anything your heart desires. With royal icing transfers, the possibilities are endless.

BIRD EYES WITH BEAK
Pipe one eye with white icing and add a black edible pearl. Allow to dry for 20 minutes before repeating for the other eye. Allow to dry completely. Pipe a yellow beak touching the bottom of the eyes and allow to dry.

TEDDY BEAR
Pipe the legs, arms and ears of the teddy bear with brown icing. Allow to dry for about 20 minutes. Pipe the head and allow to dry for 20 minutes. Pipe the tummy and allow to dry completely. Draw on eyes, mouth and belly button with a food-colour pen.

ROUND EYES
Pipe a circle with white icing using the templates for each size below. Add a black edible pearl while the icing is wet.

Small Eyes

Medium Eyes

Large Eyes

OWL EYES WITH BEAK

Pipe white circles using the template below and add black edible pearls to the centres. Allow to dry completely then pipe a yellow beak, again following the template.

TIGER EYES

Pipe the eyes with black royal icing using the template below. Add white edible pearls for the pupils.

LARGE TEXTURED EYES

Pipe a circle with black icing using the Black Centre template below. Allow the black centre to dry for several days. Pipe a circle with white icing using the White Outer template and add the dry black transfer to the centre.

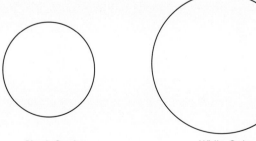

Black Centre   White Outer

ACORN

Acorns are a cute addition to a woodland-themed cookie display. Pipe the bottom section of the acorn in tan icing and allow to dry completely. Pipe the top section with brown icing and again allow to dry completely.

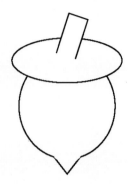

NOSES

Pipe the various nose styles using the templates provided with black or coloured icing and leave to dry completely. When black icing dries, it can look very dull. If you have an airbrush gun, you can spray the noses black before you remove them from the wax paper.

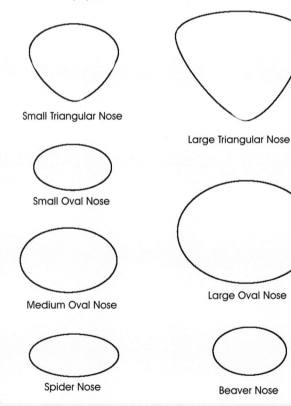

Small Triangular Nose

Large Triangular Nose

Small Oval Nose

Medium Oval Nose

Large Oval Nose

Spider Nose

Beaver Nose

Koala Nose

Heart Nose

Squirrel Nose

TEETH

Pipe a single tooth with white icing using the templates below. Allow to dry for about 20 minutes before piping the second tooth. Piping one tooth at a time will make the white icing look like two separate teeth instead of a single, wide tooth.

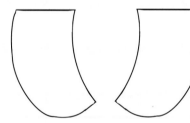

Sabre-Toothed Tiger and Woolly Mammoth Teeth

Donkey and Squirrel Teeth

Bat Fangs

Beaver Teeth

BEAKS

Pipe the beaks by following the templates below. The colours are listed beside each beak.

Duck Beak: orange Icing

Seagull Beak: yellow Icing

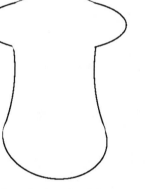

Pelican Beak: yellow Icing

Penguin and Colourful Bird Beak

Puffin beaks: Pipe the back of the beak with teal icing and the tip of the beak with orange icing. Allow to dry completely. Pipe the centre with yellow icing and allow to dry completely.

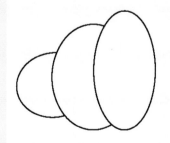

Puffin Beak

Animal Print Cookies

Animal prints are great for making large platters of cookies. They are what I call 'fill-in cookies' because you can make a lot of them in a short amount of time. If I need a platter of jungle cookies, I make a few animal cookies that will be the stars of the platter and then I fill in the platter with animal print cookies. These will save you a lot of decorating time. Any shape, size or flavour of base cookie can be used for animal print cookies.

LEOPARD PRINT

SUPPLIES

- ◆ Piping bag and nozzle
- ◆ Tan royal icing
- ◆ Brown royal icing
- ◆ Black royal icing

1. Outline and flood the cookie with tan icing.

2. While the tan icing is still wet, pipe spots with wavy edges using brown icing.

3. Outline each brown dot with a broken line using black icing and add a few black dots. Allow to dry completely.

GIRAFFE PRINT

SUPPLIES

- ◆ Piping bag and nozzle
- ◆ Yellow royal icing (yellow food colour gel mixed with a little ivory food colour gel to tone the brightness)

1. Outline and flood the cookie with a thin layer of yellow icing (keeping the layer thin will ensure that the icing does not run off the edges when the brown spots are added).

2. While the yellow icing is still wet, pipe large spots with uneven edges using tan icing. Allow to dry completely.

ZEBRA PRINT

SUPPLIES

- ◆ Piping bag and nozzle
- ◆ White royal icing
- ◆ Black royal icing

1. Outline and flood the cookie with white icing and allow to dry completely.

2. Pipe wave-like stripes using black icing – the key to a good zebra print is to make the stripes different sizes and vary the direction of the wave. Allow to dry completely.

COW PRINT	ELEPHANT PRINT	TIGER PRINT

SUPPLIES

- ◆ Piping bag and nozzle
- ◆ White royal icing
- ◆ Black royal icing

SUPPLIES

- ◆ Piping bag and nozzle
- ◆ Grey royal icing
- ◆ Brown royal icing
- ◆ Food safe paintbrush

SUPPLIES

- ◆ Piping bag and nozzle
- ◆ Orange royal icing (orange food colour gel mixed with a little ivory food colour gel to tone down the orange brightness)

COW PRINT

1. Outline and flood a cookie with white icing and allow to dry completely.

2. Pipe large spots with uneven edges using black icing. Allow to dry completely.

ELEPHANT PRINT

1. Outline the cookie with grey icing.

2. Pipe lines to resemble the lines on an elephant trunk with grey icing. Allow to dry for about 20 minutes.

3. Flood the cookie in between the lines.

4. Mix the brown icing with a little water until it is the consistency of milk. Paint the thin brown icing over the grey icing – be careful not to oversaturate the cookie (oversaturation with watered-down icing can cause holes to form in the base coat). If you do apply too much, dab off the excess with a piece of kitchen towel. Allow to dry completely.

TIGER PRINT

1. Outline and flood the cookie with orange icing and allow to dry completely.

2. Pipe wave-like stripes using black icing – the key to a good tiger print is to make the stripes different sizes and vary the direction of the wave. Allow to dry completely.

Farm & Pets

Standing Duck

A cookie cutter in the shape of a figure 8 (or a snowman) and a heart cookie cutter are used here to create a cute stand-up duck. Before baking, trim the bottom of the number 8 (or snowman) cookie so it will stand flat once baked. If the cookie spreads while baking you can shave the bottom with a handheld grater (see the Stand-up Cookies techniques on page 14).

SUPPLIES

♦ Number 8 cookie cutter or snowman cookie cutter

♦ Heart cookie cutter

♦ Piping bag and nozzle

♦ Yellow royal icing

♦ Black edible pearls

♦ Orange royal icing

♦ Orange royal icing beak (optional)

1. Choose a basic cookie recipe on pages 7–8, and make a batch of cookies using a number 8 or snowman cookie cutter, and an equal number of cookies using a heart cookie cutter. Allow the cookies to cool completely before decorating.

2. Outline the duck shape on the number 8 or snowman cookie with a wavy line using the yellow icing, and flood it. While the icing is still wet, add the black edible pearls for the eyes.

3. To create the beak, either let the yellow icing dry for a few hours then pipe a beak using the orange icing, or drop on a royal icing transfer beak (see page 17) while the yellow icing is still wet.

4. Outline and flood the feet shape on the heart cookie using orange icing. Allow both cookies to dry completely.

5. To assemble, stand the duck on the feet and pipe a little orange icing where the cookies meet to secure them together. Support the cookies in position until the icing dries (see page 14).

TIPS & TRICKS

With a little imagination, a simple cookie cutter shape can be made into something unique. I also use a heart cookie cutter to make the Swan on page 28, a star cookie cutter for the Fox on page 70, and a circle to make the Pig Face on page 27. See what cutter shapes you have in your kitchen and turn them upside down, sideways, chop pieces off, or combine them to expand on the animals you can create.

A Flock of Sheep

If you live in an area with high humidity like I do, you will need to be creative when making black and white iced cookies. This is a perfect way to think outside of the box and use multiple cookies to achieve the look you want without worrying about your icing colours running together.

SUPPLIES

- ◆ Gingerbread man cookie cutter
- ◆ Large flower cookie cutter
- ◆ Piping bag and nozzle
- ◆ Black royal icing
- ◆ White royal icing
- ◆ Small royal icing eyes (see page 15)

1. Choose a basic cookie recipe on pages 7–8, and make a batch of cookies using a gingerbread man cookie cutter. Before baking, cut the gingerbread body off below the arms in a curve, then turn the cookies upside down to make the sheep's head. Make an equal number of large flower cookies to create the sheep's body. Allow the cookies to cool completely before decorating.

2. Outline and flood the sheep's head with the black icing. Add the royal icing eyes while the icing is still wet. Set aside to dry.

3. Outline and flood two of the flower petals with the black icing.

4. Outline and flood the remaining petals with white icing.

5. While the icing is still wet, place the head in the centre of the body and set aside to dry completely.

Cow Face

One of my favourite cookie cutters for animal shapes is a bus cutter I bought from Karen's Cookies (see Suppliers on page 144). It is one of the most versatile cutters I have ever owned. To make the cow base cookies choose a basic cookie recipe on pages 7–8, then use the bus cutter to make a batch of cookies. Allow the cookies to cool completely before decorating.

SUPPLIES

- ♦ Bus cookie cutter
- ♦ Piping bag and nozzle
- ♦ White royal icing
- ♦ Large royal icing eyes (see page 15)
- ♦ Black royal icing
- ♦ Tan royal icing
- ♦ Brown royal icing
- ♦ Black food-colour pen
- ♦ Pink food-colour pen

1

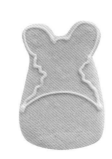

Trim the sides of the bus cookies before baking, as pictured. Once cool, outline the cow's face with white icing.

2

Flood the face with white icing and add the royal icing eyes. Allow to dry completely.

3

Outline and flood the cheek spots with black icing. Outline and flood the nose with tan icing and add two brown icing dots while the tan icing is still wet.

4

Outline and flood the hair using black icing. Draw on the ears using black and pink food-colour pens. Allow to dry completely.

Horse Face

Just like the Cow Face on pages 24–25, the base cookie for the Horse Face is made from the very versatile bus cutter from Karen's Cookies (see Suppliers on page 144).

Goat Face

A simple bat cookie cutter is used here to make a goat face cookie. If you want to make a full-body goat but do not have a goat cutter, you can use a deer cutter instead.

SUPPLIES

♦ Bus cookie cutter

♦ Piping bag and nozzle

♦ White royal icing

♦ Tan royal icing

♦ Dark brown royal icing

♦ Large black edible pearls

♦ Pink royal icing

1. Choose a basic cookie recipe on pages 7–8, and make a batch of cookies using a bus cookie cutter. Trim the sides of the bus cookies before baking. Allow the cookies to cool completely before decorating.

2. Once cool, outline and flood a stripe down the centre of the horse's face using white icing and allow to dry completely.

3. Outline and flood the nose using tan icing and pipe two dark brown ovals for the nostrils while the tan icing is still wet. Allow to dry completely.

4. Outline and flood the sides of the face and the tips of the ears with dark brown icing. Outline the sides of the ears with dark brown icing. Add the edible pearl eyes while the icing is wet.

5. Flood the inside of the ears with pink icing. Allow to dry completely.

SUPPLIES

♦ Bat cookie cutter

♦ Piping bag and nozzle

♦ Dark brown or tan royal icing

♦ Black edible pearls

♦ Royal icing heart nose (see page 17)

♦ Pink royal icing

♦ White royal icing

1. Choose a basic cookie recipe on pages 7–8, and make a batch of cookies using a bat cookie cutter. Allow the cookies to cool completely before decorating.

2. Outline and flood the head and top of the ears with dark brown or tan icing. Add the black edible pearls and the royal icing heart nose while the icing is wet. Allow to dry completely.

3. Outline and flood the inside of the ear with pink icing. Pipe horns onto the head using white icing. Allow to dry completely.

Pig

The trick with pig cookies is to keep the pink base colour very subtle. Add gel colour (see page 13) to the royal icing a little at a time to achieve the desired shade.

SUPPLIES

- ♦ Pig cookie cutter
- ♦ Piping bag and nozzle
- ♦ Pink royal icing
- ♦ Black edible pearl
- ♦ Tan royal icing

1. Choose a basic cookie recipe on pages 7–8, and make a batch of cookies using a pig cookie cutter. Allow the cookies to cool completely before decorating.

2. Outline and flood the pig with pink icing and add the black pearl eye while the icing is still wet.

3. To make the fleshy pink colour for the spots, mix tan icing, a little at a time, into pink icing. Add the pink-brown dots to the pig's back while the pink icing is still wet.

4. Pipe a curly pig tail with pink icing. Allow to dry completely.

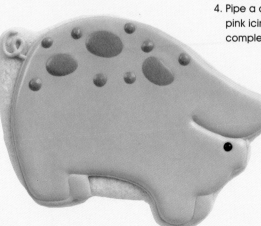

Pig Face

I like to bake circular base cookies in different sizes and freeze them so they can be grabbed when I need cookies in a hurry.

SUPPLIES

- ♦ Circle cookie cutter
- ♦ Piping bag and nozzle
- ♦ Brown food-colour pen
- ♦ Pink royal icing
- ♦ Large royal icing eyes (see page 15)
- ♦ Tan royal icing
- ♦ Black food-colour pen

1. Choose a basic cookie recipe on pages 7–8, and make a batch of cookies using a circle cookie cutter. Allow the cookies to cool completely before decorating.

2. Draw the snout and ears onto the base cookie with a brown food-colour pen.

3. Outline and flood the face with pink icing, but do not flood the ears and snout. Add the royal icing eyes while the icing is still wet. Allow to dry for 20 minutes.

4. Flood the snout and ears with pink icing, building up the icing so it rises above the face. While the snout is still wet, pipe two tan dots for the nostrils. Allow to dry completely.

5. Draw a mouth with a black food-colour pen, and draw two eyebrows with the brown food-colour pen.

A Bevy of Swans

You can use any size heart cookie cutter to make the base cookie for the swans. Simply use a heart cutter to make a batch of heart-shaped cookies, using a basic cookie recipe on pages 7–8. Allow the cookies to cool completely before decorating. For a bevy of swans, use various sizes of heart cutters.

SUPPLIES

- Heart cookie cutter
- Yellow food-colour pen
- Piping bag
- No. 2 piping nozzle
- White royal icing
- No. 10 or no. 12 piping nozzle
- Thick white icing (see page 13)
- Yellow food colour gel
- Black food colour gel
- No. 10/0 food safe paintbrush

1

Draw the swan design onto the base cookies with a yellow food-colour pen. Outline the swan using the no. 2 piping nozzle and white royal icing.

2

Using the thick white icing and a no. 10 or no. 12 piping nozzle, create the feathers by squeezing out a dot of icing and then pulling the piping bag down and towards the swan's head as you release pressure. Repeat to create 7 feathers.

3

Let the first row dry for about an hour before repeating to create 5 feathers for the second row. Allow to dry for about an hour.

4

Use the white royal icing and the no. 2 piping nozzle to outline and flood the final row of feathers.

5

Flood the swan body, neck, and head with the white royal icing. Allow to dry completely.

6

Mix a little water with a drop of yellow food colour gel and paint on the beak. Mix a little water with a drop of black food colour gel and paint a triangle on the swan's face and add a dot for the eye.

Cockerel

Cockerels come in many shapes and sizes, and so do cockerel cookies. I have made a very simple cockerel here, but you can easily use different colours for the tail feathers and even work patterns into the design using a cocktail stick.

SUPPLIES

- ◆ Cockerel cookie cutter
- ◆ Piping bag and nozzle
- ◆ White royal icing
- ◆ Medium royal icing eye (see page 15)
- ◆ Yellow royal icing
- ◆ Red royal icing

1. Choose a basic cookie recipe on pages 7–8, and make a batch of cookies using a cockerel cutter. Allow the cookies to cool completely before decorating.

2. Outline and flood the body and tail feathers with white icing. Or, to make the tail feathers really stand out, pipe them individually instead of flooding that portion of the cookie.

3. Add the royal icing eye while the white icing is still wet. Allow to dry completely.

4. Pipe the legs and feet using yellow icing, then pipe the beak with yellow icing and allow to dry for about 20 minutes.

5. Pipe the comb and wattle with red icing and allow to dry completely.

TIPS & TRICKS

Make a whole farmyard of cockerels by decorating them in different colours and styles. Practise the wet-on-wet technique (see page 14) by flooding the tail feathers and adding coloured dots. Then, while the icing is still wet, pull a cocktail stick through the dots to give a feather effect.

Chicken

Ann Clark is a Vermont-based cookie decorator who also makes cookie cutters (see Suppliers on page 144). I own several of them. This chicken was the first cutter in my Ann Clark collection. The shapes are very easy to decorate and I cannot wait to get my hands on more.

SUPPLIES

- ◆ Chicken cookie cutter
- ◆ Piping bag and nozzle
- ◆ Black royal icing
- ◆ Small royal icing eye (see page 15)
- ◆ White royal icing
- ◆ Yellow royal icing
- ◆ Red royal icing

1. Choose a basic cookie recipe on pages 7–8, and make a batch of cookies using a chicken cutter. Allow the cookies to cool completely before decorating.

2. Outline and flood the body and tail feathers with black icing.

3. Add a royal icing eye and a few white dots to the tail feathers while the black icing is still wet. Allow to dry for about 20 minutes.

4. Pipe the beak with yellow icing and allow to dry for about 20 minutes.

5. Pipe the comb and wattle with red icing and allow to dry completely.

6. Outline the wing with black icing and allow to dry for a few minutes. Flood the wing and add white dots to the feathers while the black icing is still wet. Allow to dry completely.

A Drove of Donkeys

To make the base cookie, use a flip-flop cookie cutter to cut a batch of face shapes and a rabbit cookie cutter to cut double the number of ears (so you will have 2 ears for every face shape) from raw cookie dough. Choose a basic cookie recipe on pages 7–8. Before baking, attach the rabbit ears at the narrow end of the flip-flop.

SUPPLIES

- ♦ Flip-flop cookie cutter
- ♦ Rabbit cookie cutter
- ♦ Piping bag and nozzle
- ♦ Grey royal icing
- ♦ Pink royal icing
- ♦ Black royal icing
- ♦ Black food-colour pen
- ♦ White royal icing
- ♦ Black edible pearls

1

Outline the donkey's face and top of the ears with grey icing. Outline and flood the mouth with black icing. Outline and flood the bottom of the ears with pink icing and allow to dry for several hours.

2

Flood the face and top of the ears with grey icing. While the icing is wet, pipe 2 black nostrils on the nose and allow to dry completely.

3

Draw on the top of the ears, the eyebrows, and the outline of the face using a black food-colour pen.

4

Pipe the first tooth with white icing and allow to dry for 20 minutes before piping the second. Pipe and flood 2 crescent shapes with white icing for the eyes and add the black pearls while the icing is still wet. Allow to dry completely.

TIPS & TRICKS

Instead of piping the eyes and teeth onto the donkey, you can use the pattern for the royal icing eyes and teeth on pages 15–17.

Crow

Did you know that crows are considered to be among the world's most intelligent animals? They are believed to be almost as smart as apes. Crow species have been known to construct tools from twigs and other items in order to reach food. Now that is one smart bird.

SUPPLIES

- ♦ Candy corn cookie cutter
- ♦ Piping bag and nozzle
- ♦ Black royal icing
- ♦ Royal icing bird eyes with beak (see page 15)

1. Choose a basic cookie recipe on pages 7–8, and make a batch of cookies using a candy corn cutter. Allow the cookies to cool completely before decorating.

2. Outline and flood the crow using black icing.

3. Add the royal icing eyes and beak while the black icing is still wet. Allow to dry completely.

TIPS & TRICKS

Cookies like this are a fun way to get the kids involved. You only need one colour of icing and you can give them the royal icing transfer to decorate with.

Dog

Dog cookie cutters come in many shapes and sizes and are easily found at most good cake decorating suppliers. However, I like to use a baby cutter turned upside down to make the base for my dog cookies because it creates just the right shape.

SUPPLIES

- Baby cookie cutter
- Piping bag and nozzle
- Tan royal icing
- Red royal icing
- Small black edible pearls
- Large black edible pearl

1. Choose a basic cookie recipe on pages 7–8, and make a batch of cookies using a baby cookie cutter. Before baking the cookies, cut the head off above the ears. Allow the cookies to cool completely before decorating.

2. Turn the baby cookie upside down. Outline the dog shape and flood the two back legs with tan icing. Allow to dry for 20 minutes.

3. Flood one front leg with tan icing and allow to dry for 20 minutes.

4. Repeat for the other front leg.

5. Flood the head with tan icing and add the black pearl eyes and nose while the icing is still wet. Allow to dry for several hours.

6. Outline and flood the collar with red icing. Allow to dry completely.

TIPS & TRICKS

If you are looking for accent cookies for your furry little friends, why not make sticks, balls, bones or dog houses to add to the plate?

A Herd of Bunnies

The base of the bunny cookie is made using a circle cutter and a small heart cutter. Choose a basic cookie recipe on pages 7–8, then cut a batch of circular cookies using a circle cookie cutter and cut half the number of small heart cookies. Before baking, cut each circle in half and trim the pointed end of the heart cookies with a sharp knife. Attach the 'ears' to the rounded top of the semicircles.

SUPPLIES

- ◆ Small heart cookie cutter
- ◆ Medium or large circle cookie cutter
- ◆ Piping bag and nozzle
- ◆ White royal icing
- ◆ Pink edible glitter
- ◆ Red royal icing
- ◆ Pink pearl dust
- ◆ Food safe paintbrush
- ◆ Black food-colour pen

1

Outline the bunny ears and head with white icing.

2

Flood one ear with white icing and allow to dry for 10 minutes before flooding the second ear. Again allow to dry for 10 minutes.

3

Flood the head with white icing and allow to dry overnight. Repeat steps 1–3 on the other side of the cookie so both sides are flooded with white icing.

4

Pipe a star shape for the tail using white icing and sprinkle with pink edible glitter while the icing is still wet. Allow to dry completely and turn the cookie over.

5

Pipe a small heart with red icing for the nose. Use a dry paintbrush to gently rub the pink pearl dust onto the ears and the cheeks of the bunny. Shake off the excesses. Draw the mouth and eyes with a black food-colour pen.

Yellow Cat

One day a yellow cat appeared in my yard. He was very sweet but a few days later he disappeared as quickly as he had arrived. I made this cookie as a little reminder of his visit.

SUPPLIES

♦ Cat face cookie cutter
♦ Piping bag and nozzle
♦ Yellow royal icing
♦ Orange royal icing
♦ Medium royal icing eyes (see page 15)
♦ Medium oval royal icing nose (see page 16)
♦ Black food-colour pen

1. Choose a basic cookie recipe on pages 7–8, and make a batch of cookies using a cat face cutter. Allow the cookies to cool completely before decorating.

2. Outline and flood the cat's face with yellow icing.

3. While the yellow icing is still wet, pipe stripes on the face using orange icing. Add the royal icing eyes and royal icing nose and allow to dry completely.

4. Draw the whiskers with a black food-colour pen.

Grey Cat

Once I had made the yellow cat cookie, I decided he needed a friend. I do not have any cats but with this simple design I can have cat cookies anytime I want.

SUPPLIES

♦ Cat face cookie cutter
♦ Piping bag and nozzle
♦ Grey royal icing
♦ Pink royal icing
♦ Medium royal icing eyes (see page 15)
♦ Medium oval royal icing nose (see page 16)
♦ Black food-colour pen

1. Choose a basic cookie recipe on pages 7–8, and make a batch of cookies using a cat face cutter. Allow the cookies to cool completely before decorating.

2. Outline and flood the cat's face with grey icing.

3. While the grey icing is still wet, add the royal icing eyes and royal icing nose. Allow to dry completely.

4. Flood the inside of the cat's ears with pink icing. Draw the whiskers with a black food-colour pen.

Dog Face

If you want to create a lot of dog cookies in a short amount of time, then this cookie is for you. You can make the royal icing transfer noses and eyes in advance so when it is time to decorate, simply apply the base coat of icing and then just drop on the details.

SUPPLIES

- ◆ Dog face cookie cutter
- ◆ Piping bag and nozzle
- ◆ Tan royal icing
- ◆ Black royal icing
- ◆ Medium royal icing eyes (see page 15)
- ◆ Large triangular royal icing nose (see page 16)
- ◆ Black food-colour pen

1. Choose a basic cookie recipe on pages 7–8, and make a batch of cookies using a dog face cookie cutter. Allow the cookies to cool completely before decorating.

2. Outline and flood the dog face and chin with tan icing, but do not flood the mouth. Add the royal icing eyes and nose while the tan icing is still wet.

3. Add a drop of black icing for the mouth and allow to dry completely.

4. Add a few dots to each side of the nose with a black food-colour pen.

Garden Critters

Snail

Snails are not the cutest garden creatures. In reality, they are slimy and can be a pest in the garden. The good thing about making cookies is you can take something fairly unattractive and make it wonderful. The shells of these cookies look great decorated with sweets and sprinkles.

SUPPLIES

♦ Snail cookie cutter
♦ Blue royal icing
♦ Piping bag
♦ No. 3 piping nozzle
♦ Airbrush gun with blue airbrush colour
♦ Yellow royal icing
♦ Small black edible pearls
♦ Pink royal icing

1. Choose a basic cookie recipe on pages 7–8, and make a batch of cookies using a snail cutter. Allow the cookies to cool completely before decorating.

2. Pipe a swirl of blue icing onto the back of the snail using a no. 3 piping nozzle and allow to dry for a few minutes.

3. Flood the shell with blue icing, making sure not to flood over the swirl pattern.

4. Spray the blue icing swirl on the shell with the blue airbrush colour. Hold the gun about 2.5cm (1in) away from the cookie. Start in the centre and work towards the edge of the cookie. Allow to dry completely. (For more detailed airbrush gun instructions, see page 14.)

5. Outline and flood the snail head and body with yellow icing, piping a wavy line for the bottom of the snail body.

6. Add the black edible pearl eyes while the yellow icing is still wet, and pipe two pink dots for the cheeks. Allow to dry completely.

TIPS & TRICKS

To create a shell with definition, pipe the outline and the swirl and allow to dry for a few minutes. Carefully flood the shell without covering the outline. Once the icing is dry, shade the shell or use stencils to make cute designs.

A Flight of Butterflies

This is a great cookie to customise and get creative. The wings can be a solid colour or you can use a wet-on-wet technique (see page 14) to make different designs, such as realistic butterflies with intricately decorated wings. If you are baking with children, set out bowls of sweets and sprinkles and watch them bring their butterflies to life.

SUPPLIES

- ◆ Butterfly cookie cutter
- ◆ Piping bag and nozzle
- ◆ Lime green royal icing
- ◆ Airbrush gun with green and blue airbrush colours
- ◆ Light blue royal icing
- ◆ White royal icing

1. Choose a basic cookie recipe on pages 7–8, and make a batch of cookies using a butterfly cutter. Allow the cookies to cool completely before decorating.

2. Outline and flood the butterfly wings with lime green icing and allow to dry completely.

3. Outline the edges of the wings with the green airbrush colour by holding the gun about 2.5cm (1in) away from the cookie and gently pulling the trigger. Remember, if you need to stop, let go of the trigger first so you do not get a messy spot. (For more details on how to use an airbrush gun, see page 14.)

4. Pipe the butterfly body in sections with light blue icing. Pipe alternate sections and let them dry for 20 minutes before filling in the gaps in between. Allow to dry for several hours.

5. Pipe a white line around the edge of the wings, and ovals and dots in the centres. Allow to dry completely.

A Loveliness of Ladybirds

Use a circle cookie cutter for this ladybird. Cut a batch of circular cookies using a basic cookie recipe from pages 7–8, and trim off the bottom edge of the circle before baking. You will need a little more than a half circle for this cookie to give the ladybird space to wiggle its feet.

SUPPLIES

- ◆ Circle cookie cutter
- ◆ Piping bag and nozzle
- ◆ Red royal icing
- ◆ Circle stencils
- ◆ Black food-colour pen
- ◆ Black royal icing
- ◆ 1 small and 1 medium royal icing eyes (see page 15)

1

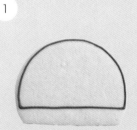

Outline a half circle onto your base cookie with red icing.

2

Flood the ladybird body with red icing and allow to dry for several hours or overnight.

3

Draw the black circles using a circle stencil and a black food-colour pen – draw circles of different sizes and position them randomly.

4

Pipe an oval shape for the ladybird's head, 2 antenna and 6 legs with black icing.

5

Add the royal icing eyes while the icing on the head is still wet and allow to dry completely.

Caterpillar

There are many caterpillar cookie cutters available – all of them are adorable and create base cookies that are fun to decorate. Customise your caterpillars by adding edible pearls and sprinkles, or use edible food-colour pens to draw on stripes and dots.

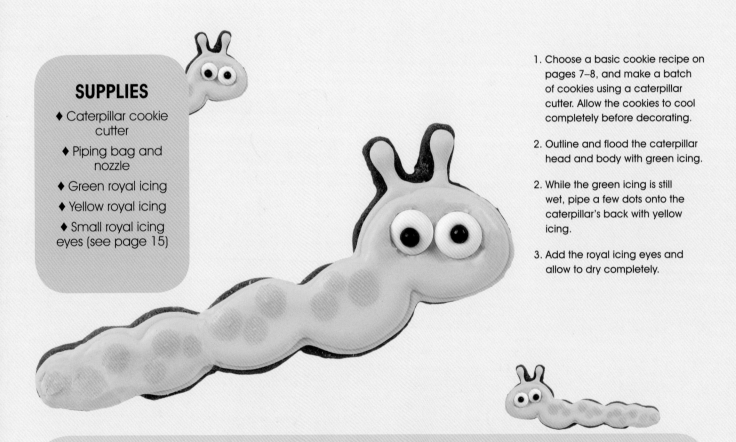

SUPPLIES

♦ Caterpillar cookie cutter

♦ Piping bag and nozzle

♦ Green royal icing

♦ Yellow royal icing

♦ Small royal icing eyes (see page 15)

1. Choose a basic cookie recipe on pages 7–8, and make a batch of cookies using a caterpillar cutter. Allow the cookies to cool completely before decorating.

2. Outline and flood the caterpillar head and body with green icing.

2. While the green icing is still wet, pipe a few dots onto the caterpillar's back with yellow icing.

3. Add the royal icing eyes and allow to dry completely.

TIPS & TRICKS

The variations for caterpillar cookies are endless. You can decorate them with one colour of icing or multiple colours. You can draw designs with food-colour pens or add sanding sugar. You can also make spots and patterns on the back with your favourite sweets. Let your imagination run wild.

Spider Face

Not all spider cookies have to be scary. You can make them cute with multiple eyes and big noses, or add sprinkles or sanding sugar to make them look hairy.

SUPPLIES

♦ Spider cookie cutter

♦ Piping bag and nozzle

♦ Black royal icing

♦ Large royal icing eyes (see page 15)

♦ Small triangular royal icing nose (see page 16)

♦ Black sanding sugar

1. Choose a basic cookie recipe on pages 7–8, and make a batch of cookies using a spider cutter. Allow the cookies to cool completely before decorating.

2. Outline and flood the spider body with black icing. Add the royal icing eyes and nose while the icing is still wet.

3. Quickly sprinkle the body with black sanding sugar while the icing is still wet. (You need to work fast in order for the sanding sugar to stick.)

4. Pipe four legs on each side of the body with black icing and sprinkle with black sanding sugar while the icing is still wet. Allow to dry completely.

Worm

Use these wriggly worms to create a garden scene with multiple cookies, or pair them with fish cookies as a gift for a fishing enthusiast.

1. Choose a basic cookie recipe on pages 7–8, and make a batch of cookies using a worm cutter. Allow the cookies to cool completely before decorating.

2. Outline the worm with reddish-brown icing and pipe three sections for the neck.

3. Flood the centre neck section and the head and tail with reddish-brown icing.

4. Add the royal icing eye while the icing is still wet and allow to dry for 20 minutes.

5. Flood the remaining neck sections and allow to dry completely.

SUPPLIES

♦ Worm cookie cutter

♦ Piping bag and nozzle

♦ Reddish-brown royal icing

♦ Medium royal icing eye (see page 15)

Frog

This fat-bellied frog is simply made using a frog cookie cutter. Bake a batch of frog base cookies using your favourite recipe from pages 7–8. I like to flood the different sections individually so the features stand out, but you can outline the edge and flood the whole cookie in one step.

1

Outline the body and legs of the frog with green icing. Flood one of the front legs with green icing.

2

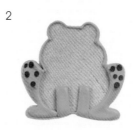

Flood the back legs with green icing. While the icing is still wet, pipe dots onto the back legs using brown icing and allow to dry for 20 minutes. Flood the other front leg and allow to dry for 20 minutes more.

3

Flood the head and body with green icing. While the icing is still wet, pipe dots onto the cheeks and the top of the head using brown icing. Add the royal icing eyes and allow to dry for 20 minutes.

4

Pipe 3 dots onto the base of each front leg for the toes. Pipe the outside toes first and allow to dry for a few minutes before piping the centre toes (this will prevent the icing from running). Allow to dry completely. Draw a smile onto the face using a black food-colour pen.

Lizard

This lizard cookie is an overhead view with the lizard looking at you – it is as if he is saying, 'You have seen me down here, haven't you?' To make him stand out even more, you could add stripes or spots on his back using a food-colour pen or different coloured royal icing.

SUPPLIES

- ♦ Lizard cookie cutter
- ♦ Piping bag and nozzle
- ♦ Blue royal icing
- ♦ Small royal icing eyes (see page 15)
- ♦ Black food-colour pen

1. Choose a basic cookie recipe on pages 7–8, and make a batch of cookies using a lizard cutter. Allow the cookies to cool completely before decorating.

2. Outline and flood the lizard's head, body and tail with blue icing.

3. While the icing is still wet, add the royal icing eyes.

4. Pipe a dot for each toe using blue icing – pull the piping bag in towards the leg to make a small triangle. Pipe three toes on each foot, then connect them to the body by piping the legs. Allow to dry completely.

5. Draw a smile onto the face using a black food-colour pen.

TIPS & TRICKS

This little guy can be iced all at once or you can decorate him in sections, allowing each section to dry before piping the next, so his feet, legs and head are defined. To work on several cookies at a time, pipe the feet for the whole batch first, then move on to the legs, then the heads, and finally the bodies.

Spider

I hope these realistic cookies will not scare anyone too much! They are a little creepy, but would suit anyone who likes spiders or keeps them as pets. For a more playful spider cookie, try the Spider Face on page 47.

SUPPLIES

- ♦ Spider cookie cutter
- ♦ Piping bag and nozzle
- ♦ Black royal icing
- ♦ Red royal icing
- ♦ Black edible pearls

1. Choose a basic cookie recipe on pages 7–8, and make a batch of cookies using a spider cutter. Allow the cookies to cool completely before decorating.

2. Outline and flood a large circle with black icing for the spider's body. While the icing is still wet, pipe a red zigzag line onto the back. Allow to dry for 20 minutes.

3. Outline and flood a smaller circle with black icing for the head. Add the black pearl eyes while the icing is still wet. Allow to dry for 20 minutes.

4. Pipe the leg sections using black icing. Start by piping thick black lines closest to the body, then pipe every other section. Allow to dry for a few minutes before adding the connecting sections. Allow to dry completely.

TIPS & TRICKS

Black royal icing can taste bitter. To ensure these cookies taste as good as they look, mix brown and green royal icing together to make a dark base, then add a little black food colour gel. This should help to cut down on the bitter taste.

A Swarm of Fireflies

This adorable firefly is made using a butterfly cookie cutter. Make a batch of cookies using your favourite cookie recipe from pages 7–8, then trim the bottom wings and shape the base of the cookie into a curve before baking.

SUPPLIES

- ♦ Butterfly cookie cutter
- ♦ Piping bag and nozzle
- ♦ White royal icing
- ♦ Airbrush gun with yellow airbrush colour
- ♦ Brown food-colour pen

1

Outline and flood the firefly with white icing and allow to dry for 30 minutes.

2

Pipe a large circle of white icing for the body and allow to dry completely.

3

To make the firefly look like it is glowing, use an airbrush gun to gently spray the body of the firefly yellow. Lightly spray the centre and allow the colour to get darker as you work your way towards the edge of the circle. (For more on using an airbrush gun, see page 14.)

4

Draw the head and wings using a brown food-colour pen.

5

Draw two antennae with dots on the tips with the brown food-colour pen.

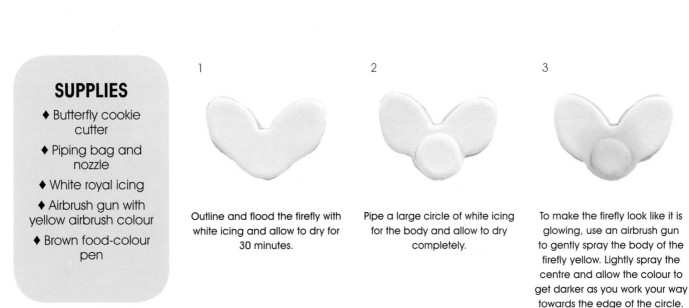

Hedgehog

I love this hedgehog cookie – he is so adorably cute and with a little pink nose, who can resist him? Make a whole batch and use them as a prop to talk to little ones about the importance of checking for hedgehogs before lighting bonfires, particularly around Bonfire Night.

SUPPLIES

♦ Hedgehog cookie cutter

♦ Piping bag and nozzle

♦ Ivory royal icing

♦ Small royal icing eye (see page 15)

♦ Brown royal icing

♦ Pink royal icing

1. Choose a basic cookie recipe on pages 7–8, and make a batch of cookies using a hedgehog cutter. Allow the cookies to cool completely before decorating.

2. Outline and flood the face and legs with ivory icing. Add the royal icing eye while the ivory icing is still wet.

3. Outline and flood the body with brown icing.

4. Pipe a circle for the nose with pink icing and allow to dry completely.

5. Pipe spikes onto the hedgehog's back using brown icing and allow to dry completely.

TIPS & TRICKS

To make the hedgehog's spikes really stand out, use homemade sprinkles. Pipe thin lines of royal icing onto wax paper and leave to dry overnight. The following day break the icing lines into pieces of varying lengths and sprinkle over the hedgehog's back at the end of step 3, while the brown icing is still wet.

Mouse

The mouse cookie is made by combining a baby cookie cutter and a star cookie cutter. The body of the mouse comes from the baby cookie cutter and the head is made with the star cookie cutter. Cut a star out of raw dough and trim the right and left arms off, so the resulting shape looks like a long pointy nose and two ears. Use the star cutter to remove the head from the baby body, place the trimmed star into the groove and bake the cookies. For more information about combining cookie cutters, see page 12.

SUPPLIES

♦ Baby cookie cutter
♦ Star cookie cutter
♦ Piping bag and nozzle
♦ Grey royal icing
♦ Pink royal icing
♦ Ivory royal icing
♦ Small black edible pearls
♦ Large black edible pearl

1. Choose a basic cookie recipe on pages 7–8, and make a batch of mouse cookies by combining baby and star cookie cutters (see above). Allow the cookies to cool completely before decorating.

2. Outline and flood the body, arms, head and the top of the ears with grey icing.

3. Pipe pink icing into the centre of each ear and allow to dry completely.

4. Pipe the feet and hands with ivory icing and leave to dry for 20 minutes.

5. Flood the face with grey icing. While the icing is wet, add the black edible pearls for the eyes and nose.

6. Pipe a tail with ivory icing and allow to dry completely.

TIPS & TRICKS

If you would prefer not to pipe the hands and feet straight onto the cookie, you can make royal icing transfers. Draw the shapes onto a piece of paper, tape it to a flat surface, cover it with wax paper and tape that down as well. Pipe the hands and feet, allow them to dry then peel them away from the wax paper.

Bee

These bee cookies are oh-so-easy to make but very effective. Made simply using a butterfly cookie cutter and decorated with sanding sugar and a food-colour pen, this is a great project for little hands to help with. Make a batch of butterfly cookies using a basic cookie recipe (see pages 7–8) and let the fun begin.

SUPPLIES

- ♦ Butterfly cookie cutter
- ♦ White royal icing
- ♦ Black sanding sugar
- ♦ Yellow sanding sugar
- ♦ Small royal icing eyes (see page 15)
- ♦ Black food-colour pen

1

Outline and flood the bee with white icing. Allow to dry completely.

2

Outline and flood 3 sections of the body with white icing, leaving even space in between each one. Sprinkle with black sanding sugar while the icing is still wet, shaking off the excess. Allow to dry for about 30 minutes.

3

Outline and flood the gaps in between the black sections with white icing. Sprinkle with yellow sanding sugar while the icing is still wet, shaking off the excess. Allow to dry for a few hours.

4

Pipe a dot of white icing onto each of the royal icing eyes and glue in place. Draw the antennae with a black food-colour pen.

Bluebird

The bluebird cookie is created in the same way as the Crow (see page 34) and the Red Cardinal (see page 79). It's a great project for kids and beginners to make because it will not matter at all if the piping is not neat. The bluebird can be decorated with homemade sprinkles (see page 14) to give it an entirely different look.

SUPPLIES

- ◆ Candy corn cookie cutter
- ◆ Piping bag and nozzle
- ◆ Blue royal icing
- ◆ Royal icing bird eyes with beak (see page 15)

1. Choose a basic cookie recipe on pages 7–8, and make a batch of cookies using the candy corn cutter. Allow the cookies to cool completely before decorating.

2. Outline and flood the bluebird using blue icing.

3. Add the royal icing eyes and beak while the blue icing is still wet. Allow to dry completely.

TIPS & TRICKS

I used candy corn, bus and heart cookie cutters to create several different designs in this book. I challenge you to grab some simple cutters, some paper and a pencil, and trace each cookie cutter several times. See how many different designs you can make from each one. You do not have to spend a lot of money on cookie cutters – you just need to think outside of its original shape.

Dragonfly

This dragonfly has airbrushed wings, but if you do not have an airbrush gun, do not worry. Instead, decorate the wings with a few dots of different coloured royal icing, or try the wet-on-wet technique (see page 14). Make a large dot on the wing and drag a cocktail stick through the middle to make a heart shape.

SUPPLIES

♦ Dragonfly cookie cutter
♦ Piping bag and nozzle
♦ Yellow food-colour pen
♦ Light green royal icing
♦ Airbrush gun with green airbrush gun colour
♦ Reddish-brown royal icing

TIPS & TRICKS

To make these cookies 'fly', use a straw to make a hole in the head or wing of the base cookie before baking. Once the cookies are decorated and completely dry, thread string through the hole and hang the cookies up.

1. Choose a basic cookie recipe on pages 7–8, and make a batch of cookies using the dragonfly cutter. Allow the cookies to cool completely before decorating.

2. Draw the wings onto the base cookie using a yellow food-colour pen.

3. Outline and flood the top wings with light green icing and allow to dry for 20 minutes.

4. Outline and flood the lower wings with the green icing and allow to dry for about an hour.

5. Outline the wings using the airbrush gun and green airbrush colour, holding the tip of the gun about 2.5cm (1in) from the cookie. (For more on using an airbrush gun, see techniques on page 14.)

6. Outline and flood the head and body with reddish-brown icing. Allow to dry completely.

Woodland Creatures

Deer

I found this cookie cutter online and I love it. It is a simple design that has easy to follow shapes. It is great for making Christmas and woodland-themed cookies. Make a batch of different-sized deer to create a whole herd of deer.

SUPPLIES

♦ Deer cookie cutter
♦ Piping bag and nozzle
♦ Tan royal icing
♦ White royal icing
♦ Black edible pearl
♦ Black food-colour pen

1. Choose a basic cookie recipe on pages 7–8, and make a batch of cookies using the deer cutter. Allow the cookies to cool completely before decorating.

2. Outline and flood the deer with tan icing.

3. While the tan icing is still wet, pipe white dots onto the deer's back and a line on the bottom of the tail using white icing.

4. Add a black edible pearl for the eye while the tan icing is still wet. Allow to dry completely.

5. Draw hooves and a nose with the black food-colour pen.

A Colony of Rabbits

Making cookies that stand up can be simple with the help of a few basic tips – follow the techniques on page 14 for Stand-up Cookies, or simply use smaller cookies as supports, as I have done here. Add support to both sides of larger cookies to ensure they remain standing.

SUPPLIES

♦ Wilton sitting rabbit cookie cutter

♦ Small heart cookie cutter

♦ Pink, blue, brown or yellow royal icing

♦ Airbrush gun and pink, blue, brown or yellow airbrush colour

♦ Ribbons in contrasting colours

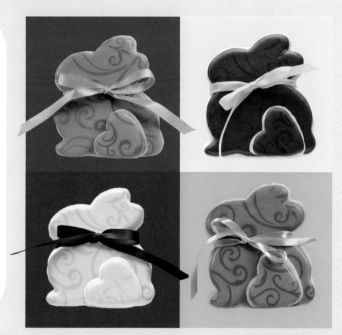

1. Choose a basic cookie recipe on pages 7–8, and make a batch of cookies using the sitting rabbit cutter and twice the number of cookies using the small heart cutter. Allow the cookies to cool completely before decorating.

2. Outline and flood the rabbit body and the heart-shaped legs with pink, blue, brown or yellow icing and allow to dry completely.

3. Airbrush a pattern onto the rabbit and each leg and allow to dry for a few hours (see page 14 for more on the airbrushing techniques). Either follow the design in the photographs or create your own. If you do not have an airbrush gun, draw on a design using food-colour pens.

4. To assemble, pipe a little icing onto the back of each leg. Line up the bottom edges of the legs with the bottom edge of the rabbit. (I usually stand the cookie on a table to make sure it is standing straight). Lay the cookie on its side and use an extra cookie to prop up the rabbit head so the body will be flat and dry without the legs sliding. Allow to dry completely.

5. Tie a ribbon around each cookie.

TIPS & TRICKS

For each rabbit you will need 1 rabbit and 2 heart cookies. Trimming the bottom of each before baking will help to ensure the cookies stand up.

Beaver

To make this cookie you will need a star cookie cutter, a frog cookie cutter and a squirrel cookie cutter. Cut a batch of cookies from your favourite cookie dough (see pages 7–8). Use the star cutter to cut off the head of the frog to make space for the star head to be attached to the body. Cut out and attach a star to the top of the frog body. Cut out a squirrel tail and attach it to the knee of the frog. The cookies are then ready to bake. For tips on combining cookie cutters, see page 12.

SUPPLIES

- ◆ Frog cookie cutter
- ◆ Star cookie cutter
- ◆ Squirrel cookie cutter
- ◆ Piping bag and nozzle
- ◆ Tan royal icing
- ◆ Dark brown royal icing
- ◆ Cream royal icing
- ◆ Black royal icing
- ◆ Large royal icing eyes (see page 15)
- ◆ Large royal icing teeth (see page 17)

1

Outline the beaver body with tan icing, the tail with dark brown icing, and the tummy with cream icing.

2

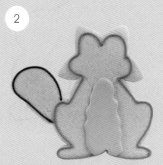

Flood the tummy with the cream icing and allow to dry for a few hours.

3

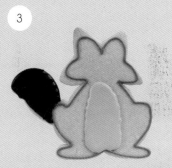

Flood the tail with dark brown icing and pipe horizontal and vertical lines with black icing.

4

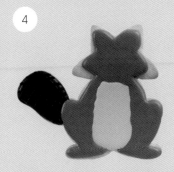

Flood the body with tan icing and allow to dry for 20 minutes.

5

Attach the royal icing eyes using a little tan icing to glue in place. Pipe a large oval of tan icing for the snout and attach the royal icing teeth and nose. Pipe the paws with tan icing and leave to dry completely.

Moose

Moose look like they would be friendly animals but they are not. They can be very aggressive and should not be approached. However, they do look a little comical and are perfect for a cookie design. I think making moose cookies is as close to a moose as I would like to get!

SUPPLIES

- ♦ Moose cookie cutter
- ♦ Piping bag and nozzle
- ♦ Dark brown icing
- ♦ Tan icing
- ♦ Black edible pearls

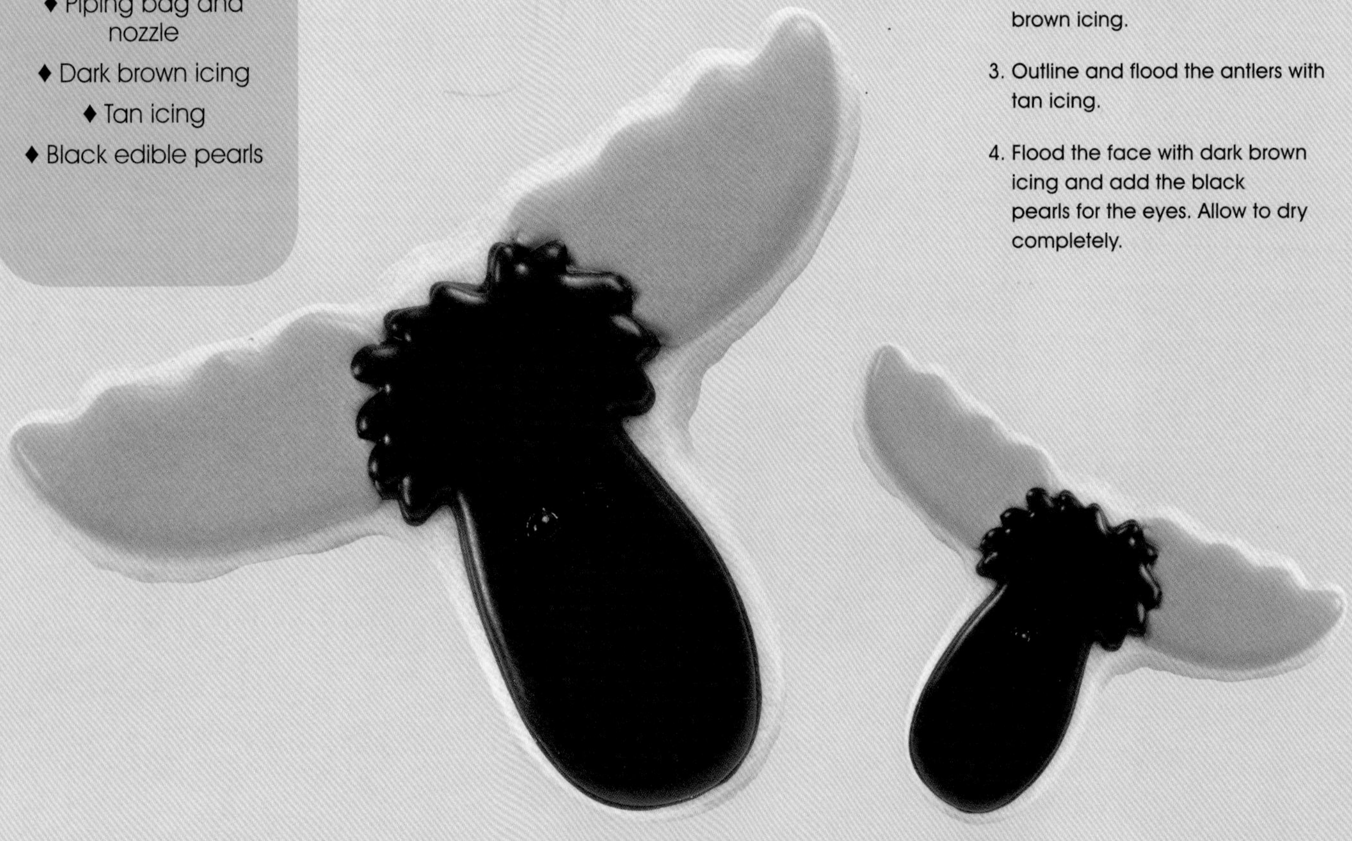

1. Choose a basic cookie recipe on pages 7–8, and make a batch of cookies using the moose cutter. Allow the cookies to cool completely before decorating.

2. Outline the moose face with dark brown icing.

3. Outline and flood the antlers with tan icing.

4. Flood the face with dark brown icing and add the black pearls for the eyes. Allow to dry completely.

Mr & Mrs Bear

We once had a bear that would visit our backyard and help itself to the corn growing in our garden. We used to make lots of noise by hitting a pot with a spoon to scare it away. Well, it worked for a while until one day he appeared with his girlfriend. I knew at that moment I had to make a Mr & Mrs Bear set of cookies.

SUPPLIES

♦ Bear face cookie cutter

♦ Piping bag and nozzle

♦ Dark brown royal icing

♦ Black edible pearls

♦ White edible pearls

♦ White royal icing

♦ Tan royal icing

♦ Small triangular royal icing noses (see page 16)

♦ Edible flower decoration

1. Choose a basic cookie recipe on pages 7–8, and make 2 cookies using the bear face cutter. Allow the cookies to cool completely before decorating.

2. Outline and flood the faces with dark brown icing. Add the black pearl eyes. For Mrs Bear, add two white edible pearls for earrings. Allow to dry for 20 minutes.

3. Flood the snouts with tan icing and add the royal icing noses while the icing is wet. Allow to dry overnight.

4. Add a dot of icing to the back of the edible flower decoration and place it in Mrs Bear's hair. Allow to dry for several hours.

A Parliament of Owls

The owl cookies are made by combining an egg cookie cutter with a heart cookie cutter. Using your choice of cookie dough from the basic recipes on pages 7–8, cut equal numbers of egg-shaped and heart-shaped cookies. Cut the tops off the egg cookies using the bottom of the egg cutter. Cut the heart cookies in half and trim them to make wing shapes. Attach a wing to either side of the owl body cookies and bake.

SUPPLIES

- ♦ Egg cookie cutter
- ♦ Heart cookie cutter
- ♦ Piping bag
- ♦ No. 2 piping nozzle
- ♦ PME 2.5 or 3 piping nozzle
- ♦ Royal icing in your choice of colours
- ♦ Table knife
- ♦ Large royal icing textured eyes (see page 16)
- ♦ Orange royal icing

1

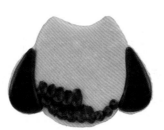

Outline and flood the wings using your choice of royal icing colour. Pipe dots along the bottom of the owl's body using a PME 2.5 or 3 nozzle. Starting in the centre of the dots, use a table knife to pull the icing dots towards the top of the cookie.

2

Continue creating rows of dots, overlapping them slightly, until you almost reach the top of the head. Pipe a line across the top of the head for the eyebrow.

3

Add the royal icing eyes while the icing is still wet. Pipe a beak and toes using orange icing. Allow to dry completely.

Fox

To make this cookie you will need a star cookie cutter, a frog cookie cutter and a squirrel cookie cutter. Cut a batch of cookies from your favourite cookie dough (see pages 7–8). Use the star cutter to cut off the head of the frog to make space for the star head to be attached to the body. Cut out and attach a star to the top of the frog body. Cut out a squirrel tail and attach it to the knee of the frog. The cookies are then ready to bake. For tips on combining cookie cutters, see page 12.

SUPPLIES

♦ Frog cookie cutter

♦ Star cookie cutter

♦ Squirrel cookie cutter

♦ Piping bag and nozzle

♦ White royal icing

♦ Rust royal icing

♦ Small black edible pearls

♦ Large black edible pearl

♦ Black food-colour pen

1. Choose a basic cookie recipe on pages 7–8, and make a batch of cookies as above. Allow the cookies to cool completely before decorating.

2. Outline and flood the cheeks, chest, and tip of the tail with white icing and allow to dry completely.

3. Outline and flood the face with the rust icing. While the icing is still wet, add the small black edible pearls for the eyes and the large black edible pearl for the nose.

4. Outline the tail, body, and legs with rust icing and allow to dry for 20 minutes.

5. Flood the tail, body, and legs with the rust icing. Allow to dry completely.

Bear Face

Sometimes the simplest cookie cutters can be used to make the base for animal cookies. Here, a heart cutter is used to make a bear face, but that is just the beginning. You can also use a heart cutter to make a dog, cat or koala. What animals can you make out of a heart cookie?

SUPPLIES

♦ Heart cookie cutter

♦ Piping bag and nozzle

♦ Dark brown royal icing

♦ Tan royal icing

♦ Medium royal icing eyes (see page 15)

♦ Large triangular royal icing nose (see page 16)

1. Choose a basic cookie recipe on pages 7–8, and make a batch of cookies using a heart cutter. Allow the cookies to cool completely before decorating.

2. Outline the bear's face and ears with dark brown icing.

3. Flood the edges of the ears and pipe tan icing into the centres. Allow to dry for 20 minutes.

4. Flood the face with the dark brown icing and add the royal icing eyes while the dark brown icing is still wet. Allow to dry for several hours.

5. Pipe the snout with tan icing and add the royal icing nose while the tan icing is wet. Allow to dry completely.

Porcupine

To make your own custom sprinkles, pipe thin lines of deep red royal icing onto wax paper and leave to dry overnight. The following day, break the icing lines into pieces of varying lengths. Store your homemade sprinkles in an airtight container in a dry place away from sunlight. Then bake a batch of hedgehog base cookies using your favourite recipe from pages 7–8 and you are all set.

SUPPLIES

- ♦ Hedgehog cookie cutter
- ♦ Piping bag and nozzle
- ♦ Tan royal icing
- ♦ Small black edible pearl
- ♦ Black royal icing
- ♦ Deep red royal icing
- ♦ Sprinkles made from deep red royal icing (see above)

1

Outline and flood the face and feet with the tan icing.

2

While the icing is still wet, add a black edible pearl for the eye. Pipe a dot of black icing for the nose and outline the body with deep red icing.

3

Outline and flood the back of the porcupine with deep red icing.

TIPS & TRICKS

To make deep red icing, mix red food colouring with a touch of brown and violet until you get the deep red you desire.

4

Add the sprinkles to the deep red icing while it is still wet. Allow to dry completely.

Raccoon

SUPPLIES

♦ Frog cookie cutter

♦ Star cookie cutter

♦ Squirrel cookie cutter

♦ Piping bag and nozzle

♦ Grey icing

♦ Small heart royal icing nose (see page 17)

♦ Black royal icing

♦ Medium royal icing eyes (see page 15)

1. To make the raccoon cookie you will need a star cookie cutter, a frog cookie cutter and a squirrel cookie cutter. Follow the instructions for the Beaver on page 65 to make the base cookie.

2. Outline and flood the top and bottom of the head (leaving an empty strip for the mask) using grey icing. Add the royal icing nose while the icing is still wet.

3. Outline and flood the tummy, arms and legs with grey icing and allow to dry for 20 minutes.

4. Outline and flood the tail with grey icing and pipe wavy lines with black icing while the grey icing is still wet.

5. Pipe the mask with black icing and add the royal icing eyes. Allow to dry completely.

Skunk

SUPPLIES

♦ Frog cookie cutter

♦ Star cookie cutter

♦ Squirrel cookie cutter

♦ Piping bag and nozzle

♦ White royal icing

♦ Small black edible pearls

♦ Black royal icing

♦ Small royal icing nose (see page 16)

1. To make the skunk cookie you will need a star cookie cutter, a frog cookie cutter and a squirrel cookie cutter. Follow the instructions for the Beaver on page 65 to make the base cookie.

2. Outline and flood the face and tail centre with white icing. Add the black pearls for the eyes while the icing is still wet. Allow to dry for 20 minutes.

3. Outline and flood the tummy with white icing. Allow to dry overnight.

4. Outline and flood the head, legs, and tail with black icing. Allow to dry for 20 minutes.

5. Flood the arms with black icing. Add a dot of icing to the back of the royal icing nose and attach it to the face. Allow to dry completely.

Squirrel

Teddy Bear

SUPPLIES

♦ Frog cookie cutter

♦ Star cookie cutter

♦ Squirrel cookie cutter

♦ Piping bag and nozzle

♦ Tan royal icing

♦ Ivory royal icing

♦ Small royal icing eyes (see page 15)

♦ Light tan royal icing

♦ Royal icing acorn (see page 16)

♦ Royal icing teeth (see page 17)

♦ Royal icing heart nose (see page 17)

1. To make the squirrel cookie you will need a star cookie cutter, a frog cookie cutter and a squirrel cookie cutter. Follow the instructions for the Beaver on page 65 to make the base cookie.

2. Outline and flood the body and tail with tan icing.

3. Outline and flood the tummy with ivory icing and allow to dry for several hours.

4. Outline and flood the head with tan icing and add the royal icing eyes while the icing is still wet. Pipe the light tan ears.

5. Add a dot of tan icing to the back of the royal icing acorn and attach it to the squirrel's tummy.

6. Pipe the cheeks using tan icing and add the royal icing teeth and royal icing nose while the tan icing is still wet.

7. Outline and flood the arms with tan icing and allow to dry completely.

SUPPLIES

♦ Baby cookie cutter

♦ Piping bag and nozzle

♦ Tan royal icing

♦ Royal icing teddy bear (see page 15)

♦ Dark tan royal icing

♦ Black edible pearls

1. Choose a basic cookie recipe on pages 7–8, and make a batch of cookies using a baby cutter. Allow the cookies to cool completely before decorating.

2. Outline the bear's ears, head, arms, body and feet in sections with tan icing.

3. Flood the ears and the body with the tan icing.

4. Add a royal icing teddy bear to the tummy while the icing is still wet. Allow to dry for 20 minutes.

5. Flood the feet and face with tan icing. While the icing is still wet, pipe the nose, mouth and paws using dark tan icing. Add the black edible pearls for the eyes. Allow to dry for 20 minutes.

6. Flood the arms with the tan icing and allow to dry completely.

Grizzly on a Campout

This cookie may look complicated but it is really quite simple. The base cookies are made by simply baking a batch of rectangles and bear faces, and double the number of small flowers, using your favourite recipe from pages 7–8. Remember to allow the cookies to cool completely before decorating.

SUPPLIES

- ♦ Rectangle cookie cutter
- ♦ Bear face cookie cutter
- ♦ Mini flower cookie cutter
- ♦ White royal icing
- ♦ Piping bag and nozzle
- ♦ Lime green royal icing
- ♦ Rust royal icing
- ♦ Yellow and black food-colour pens
- ♦ Tan royal icing
- ♦ Dark brown royal icing
- ♦ Small triangular royal icing nose (see page 16)
- ♦ Food safe paintbrush

1

First make the sleeping bag and pillow. Using a yellow food-colour pen, draw a sleeping bag pattern onto the rectangle cookie. Pipe a thin layer of lime green icing onto the top section of the sleeping bag and spread it out with the paintbrush.

2

Pipe and flood the middle section with lime green icing. Outline and flood the top and bottom sections of the sleeping bag with rust icing, then outline and flood the pillow with white icing. Allow to dry for a few hours.

3

To make the bear's head, outline and flood the snout with the tan icing and add a royal icing nose while the icing is still wet. Outline and flood the face with dark brown icing. Pipe 2 tan circles for the ears and allow to dry. Once dry, draw 2 half circles for sleepy eyes with a black food-colour pen.

4

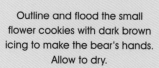

Outline and flood the small flower cookies with dark brown icing to make the bear's hands. Allow to dry.

5

Pipe a little white icing onto the backs of the bear head and paws and press in place. Allow to dry completely

Reindeer

Bat

SUPPLIES

- ♦ Reindeer head cookie cutter
- ♦ Ivory royal icing
- ♦ Airbrush gun with warm brown airbrush colour
- ♦ Tan royal icing
- ♦ Black edible pearl
- ♦ Black royal icing

1. Choose a basic cookie recipe on pages 7–8, and make a batch of cookies using the reindeer head cutter. Allow the cookies to cool completely before decorating.

2. Outline and flood the antlers with the ivory icing. Allow to dry for 20 minutes.

3. Airbrush the edges of the antlers with warm brown airbrush colour (see page 14).

4. Outline and flood the head and neck with tan icing and add a black pearl for the eye.

5. Pipe a black dot for the nose and allow to dry completely.

SUPPLIES

- ♦ Bat cookie cutter
- ♦ Purple royal icing
- ♦ Small royal icing fangs (see page 17)
- ♦ Small royal icing eyes (see page 15)
- ♦ Black food-colour pen

1. Choose a basic cookie recipe on pages 7–8, and make a batch of cookies using the bat cutter. Allow the cookies to cool completely before decorating.

2. Outline the body and wings with purple icing.

3. Flood the wings and allow to dry for 20 minutes.

4. Flood the body and add the royal icing fangs and the royal icing eyes. Allow to dry completely.

5. Draw a smile and eyebrows with a black food-colour pen.

Owl Face

SUPPLIES

♦ Bus cookie cutter
♦ Orange royal icing
♦ Black food-colour pen
♦ White royal icing
♦ Black edible pearls
♦ Yellow royal icing

1. Choose a basic cookie recipe on pages 7–8, and make a batch of cookies using the bus cutter. Trim the sides of the cookies before baking, and allow the cookies to cool completely before decorating.

2. Turn the bus base cookie upside down. Outline and flood the owl with orange icing and allow to dry completely.

3. Outline the edge of the owl with a broken line and dots using a black food-colour pen.

4. Pipe one eye with white icing and add a black edible pearl. Allot to dry for 20 minutes. Repeat for the second eye and allow to dry for a few hours.

5. Pipe the beak with yellow icing and allow to dry completely.

Red Cardinal

SUPPLIES

♦ Candy corn cookie cutter
♦ Piping bag and nozzle
♦ Red royal icing
♦ Royal icing bird eyes with beak (see page 15)

1. Choose a basic cookie recipe on pages 7–8, and make a batch of cookies using a candy corn cutter. Allow the cookies to cool completely before decorating.

2. Outline and flood the red cardinal using red icing.

3. Add the royal icing eyes with beak while the red icing is still wet. Allow to dry completely.

Ocean & Ice Animals

A Pod of Dolphins

Dolphins are one of my favourite sea animals. I only hope my quick and easy dolphin cookie can do this beautiful creature justice! A great cookie for beginner decorators, a pod of dolphins can be made in no time.

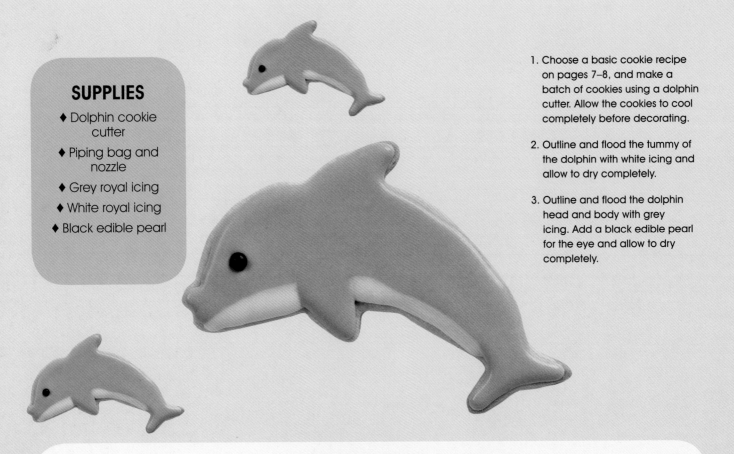

SUPPLIES

♦ Dolphin cookie cutter
♦ Piping bag and nozzle
♦ Grey royal icing
♦ White royal icing
♦ Black edible pearl

1. Choose a basic cookie recipe on pages 7–8, and make a batch of cookies using a dolphin cutter. Allow the cookies to cool completely before decorating.

2. Outline and flood the tummy of the dolphin with white icing and allow to dry completely.

3. Outline and flood the dolphin head and body with grey icing. Add a black edible pearl for the eye and allow to dry completely.

TIPS & TRICKS

To make this cookie in double quick time, it is possible to outline and flood the grey and white areas at the same time, without waiting for the white icing to dry. However, do not try this if you live in a humid area, as the icing colours may bleed into each other.

Catfish

Animal cookies can be realistic recreations, but I like mine to be humorous. In reality, catfish are not the prettiest of fish, so I have taken their name literally and have designed this cookie to look like a cat. And why not? Have fun and be creative.

SUPPLIES

♦ Angelfish cookie cutter

♦ Piping bag and nozzle

♦ White royal icing

♦ 1 small and 1 medium royal icing eyes (see page 15)

♦ Black royal icing heart nose (see page 17)

♦ Pink food colour dust

♦ Food safe paintbrush

♦ Black food-colour pen

1. Choose a basic cookie recipe on pages 7–8, and make a batch of cookies using an angelfish cutter. Allow the cookies to cool completely before decorating.

2. Turn the angelfish cookie upside down and outline and flood it with white icing.

3. While the icing is still wet, add the small royal icing eye close to the edge of the cookie and the medium royal icing eye beside it to give the illusion of the fish looking at you from a side view.

4. Add the royal icing nose and allow the cookie to dry completely.

5. Add a little pink food colour dust to the ear and cheek using the paintbrush.

6. Draw a line for a mouth and whiskers with a black food-colour pen.

Clownfish

Clownfish are actually called false anemonefish, but I think clownfish is a better description! These adorable fish are named after the multicoloured sea anemone in which they live. To make the base cookies, bake a batch of fish cookies using your favourite basic cookie recipe from pages 7–8.

SUPPLIES

♦ Fish cookie cutter
♦ Piping bag and nozzle
♦ White royal icing
♦ Orange royal icing
♦ Small royal icing eye (see page 15)

1

Outline two wavy sections on the back of the clownfish with white icing. Pipe lines of orange icing onto the fins and tail, leaving space in between each one.

2

Flood the white sections and allow to dry completely.

3

Fill in the gaps on the fins and tail by piping orange icing. Outline and flood the head with orange icing. While the icing is still wet, add a royal icing eye.

4

Flood the centre and back of the body with orange icing and allow to dry completely.

Seal

This easy project is great for getting kids involved in the kitchen. Simply bake a batch of seal base cookies using their favourite recipe from pages 7–8, help to keep little hands steady while outlining and flooding, then let them customise their creations with edible glitter and sanding sugar.

SUPPLIES

♦ Seal cookie cutter
♦ Piping bag and nozzle
♦ Grey royal icing
♦ White royal icing
♦ Black edible pearl
♦ Red edible glitter or sanding sugar

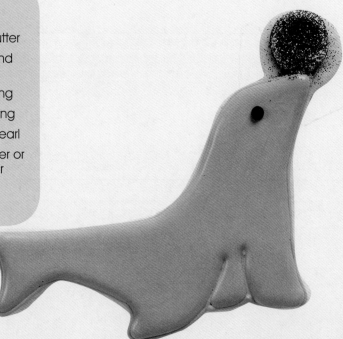

1. Choose a basic cookie recipe on pages 7–8, and make a batch of cookies using a seal cutter. Allow the cookies to cool completely before decorating.

2. Outline the seal with grey icing, adding two lines to the bottom to define the flippers.

3. Outline the ball with white icing.

4. Flood the seal with grey icing and add a black edible pearl for the eye while the icing is still wet. Allow the cookie to dry for several hours.

5. Flood the ball with white icing and sprinkle with edible glitter or sanding sugar while the icing is still wet. Allow the cookie to dry completely.

TIPS & TRICKS

I have created my seal in a true-to-life grey, but you do not have to. Get creative with colours and make a whole colony of brightly coloured seals. You do not have to limit the sparkle to the ball either – for a really shimmery cookie, sprinkle grey sanding sugar over the seal while the grey icing is still wet.

Stingray

Rays are beautiful fish who move with such grace – watching them can be captivating. This iconic creature of the deep makes a lovely cookie with its elegant shape. I like to give mine rosy cheeks for a bit of personality, but they look great plain, too.

SUPPLIES

♦ Stingray cookie cutter
♦ Piping bag and nozzle
♦ Grey royal icing
♦ White royal icing
♦ Small royal icing eyes (see page 15)
♦ Pink royal icing

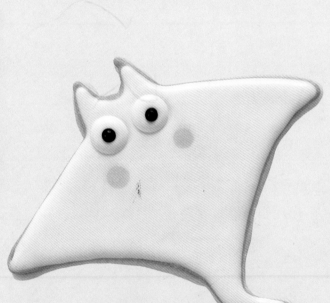

1. Choose a basic cookie recipe on pages 7–8, and make a batch of cookies using a stingray cutter. Allow the cookies to cool completely before decorating.

2. Outline the stingray with grey icing.

3. Flood the cookie with white icing and add royal icing eyes while the icing is still wet.

4. Pipe 2 pink dots for the cheeks and allow the cookie to dry completely.

TIPS & TRICKS

This cookie has a very delicate tail. If you plan on posting or transporting them, be sure to support the tails – place the cookie in a food safe bag and gently tape the bag to a piece of cardboard.

A Bloom of Jellyfish

These jellyfish cookies are so much fun to make and are sure to raise a smile. They are the perfect project for experimenting with colour and will brighten up a buffet table or children's party spread. To make the base cookies, bake a batch of jellyfish cookies using a basic cookie recipe from pages 7–8.

SUPPLIES

- ♦ Jellyfish cookie cutter
- ♦ Piping bag and nozzle
- ♦ Dark blue royal icing
- ♦ Light blue royal icing
- ♦ Black edible pearls
- ♦ Pink royal icing

1

Outline the head and pipe 4 legs with dark blue icing.

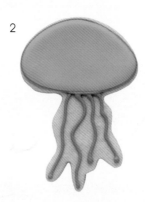

2

Flood the head with light blue royal icing.

3

While the icing is still wet, pipe a few dots or ovals to the top of the head with the dark blue icing.

4

Add the 2 black edible pearls for the eyes while the icing is still wet.

5

Pipe 2 dots with pink icing for the cheeks.

6

Pipe 4 more legs with light blue icing, overlapping the dark blue legs. Allow to dry completely.

Whale

I have used a realistic black icing and a playful green icing to decorate my whales, but you can use whatever colours you like. Animal cookies should be fun, so do not feel you have to follow traditional colours. Who knew whales would look so good in bright green?

SUPPLIES

- ◆ Whale cookie cutter
- ◆ Piping bag and nozzle
- ◆ Royal icing colours of your choice
- ◆ Large or medium royal icing eye (see page 15)

1. Choose a basic cookie recipe on pages 7–8, and make a batch of cookies using a whale cutter. Allow the cookies to cool completely before decorating.

2. Outline and flood the whales in your chosen icing colour.

3. Add a royal icing eye while the icing is wet and allow to dry completely.

TIPS & TRICKS

If you decide to use black icing to ice your whales, beware that it can have a bitter taste. See page 13 for a tip to reduce the bitterness and to help your cookies taste as good as they look.

A Shiver of Sharks

Ocean animal cookies make great cupcake toppers for sea-themed children's parties. Bake a batch of cupcakes and ice them with blue frosting – use a pallet knife to add texture and sprinkle over a little icing sugar to resemble surf – then top with shark, whale or dolphin cookies.

SUPPLIES

- ♦ Shark cookie cutter
- ♦ Piping bag and nozzle
- ♦ Grey royal icing
- ♦ Medium royal icing eye (see page 15)
- ♦ White royal icing (optional)

1. Choose a basic cookie recipe on pages 7–8, and make a batch of cookies using a shark cutter. Allow the cookies to cool completely before decorating.

2. Outline and flood the tummy of the shark with white icing and allow to dry completely.

3. Outline and flood the body with grey icing.

4. While the icing is still wet, add the royal icing eye and allow to dry completely.

5. If you want the shark to have a white tummy, follow the directions for the dolphin on page 82.

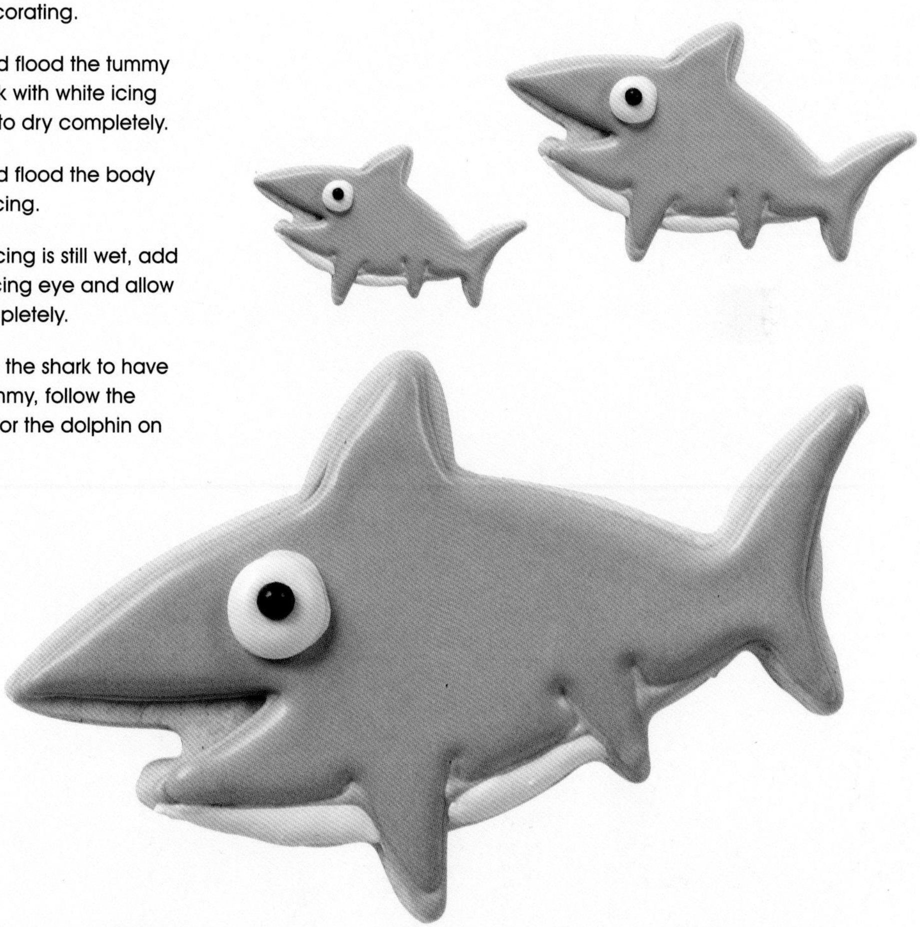

A Herd of Walruses

A candy corn cutter can be used to make so many animal designs. Simply bake a batch of candy corn cookies using your favourite cookie dough recipe from pages 7–8. You could use royal icing transfers for the cheeks and teeth to make decorating the cookies even easier.

SUPPLIES

- ◆ Candy corn cookie cutter
- ◆ Piping bag and nozzle
- ◆ Light grey royal icing
- ◆ White royal icing
- ◆ Medium grey royal icing
- ◆ Black edible pearls

1 Outline the walrus body with light grey icing. Allow to dry for several minutes.

2 Flood the body with light grey icing and allow to dry for several hours.

3 Pipe 2 eyes with white icing and add a black edible pearl to each. Pipe the cheeks with medium grey icing and add 3 edible pearls to each side. Allow to dry.

4 Pipe 2 tusks with white icing and allow to dry for several hours.

Penguin with a Hat

Who would have thought a house cookie cutter could be used to make a penguin? To create the base cookie for this chilly chick, simply cut a batch of house cookies using a basic cookie recipe from pages 7–8 and trim off the chimney before baking.

SUPPLIES

- ♦ House cookie cutter
- ♦ Piping bag and nozzle
- ♦ White royal icing
- ♦ Black edible pearls
- ♦ Orange royal icing beak (see page 17)
- ♦ Pink royal icing
- ♦ Black royal icing
- ♦ Rose or star piping nozzle
- ♦ Thick white icing (see page 13)

1. Choose a basic cookie recipe on pages 7–8, and make a batch of cookies using a house cutter. Trim off the chimneys before baking and allow the cookies to cool completely before decorating.

2. Outline and flood the middle section with white icing. Add the black edible pearls for eyes and the royal icing beak while the icing is still wet.

3. Outline and flood the hat with pink icing and allow to dry completely.

4. Outline and flood the body with black icing and allow to dry completely.

5. With a rose or star nozzle, pipe a thick white wavy line of thick white icing on the bottom of the hat and a bobble on the top.

6. Pipe the toes using orange icing and allow to dry completely.

Octopus

To make this cookie you will need to work fast. The icing technique used is wet-on-wet (see page 14) and all of the details need to be added before the icing forms a crust. If you are at all nervous about your piping technique, practise piping the design onto wax paper first.

SUPPLIES

- ◆ Pineapple cookie cutter
- ◆ Piping bag and nozzle
- ◆ Grey royal icing
- ◆ White royal icing
- ◆ White edible pearls
- ◆ Black edible pearls
- ◆ Light pink royal icing

1. Choose a basic cookie recipe on pages 7–8, and make a batch of cookies using a pineapple cutter. Allow the cookies to cool completely before decorating.

2. Outline and flood the octopus with grey icing.

3. While the grey icing is still wet, pipe ovals onto the top of the head using white icing.

4. Add the white edible pearls to the legs and the black edible pearls for the eyes. Allow to dry for 20 minutes.

5. Pipe the cheeks using the pink icing and allow to dry completely.

Sea Turtle

To make the sea turtle base cookie, cut equal numbers of candy corn and rabbit cookies from your chosen cookie dough (see pages 7–8). Before baking, trim the ears from the rabbit cookie with the rounded corner of the candy corn cutter, and place the ears firmly against the bottom corners of the candy corn cookie.

SUPPLIES

- ♦ Rabbit cookie cutter with long ears
- ♦ Candy corn cookie cutter
- ♦ Piping bag and nozzle
- ♦ Tan royal icing
- ♦ Brown royal icing
- ♦ Green royal icing
- ♦ Medium royal icing eyes (see page 15)
- ♦ Black food-colour pen

1

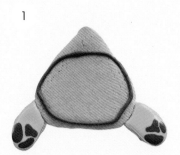

Outline the turtle shell with tan icing. Outline and flood the flippers with green icing. Pipe brown dots onto the flippers while the green icing is wet.

2

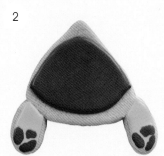

Flood the shell with the tan icing.

3

Pipe spots onto the shell with brown icing while the tan icing is still wet. Allow to dry completely.

4

Outline and flood a mushroom-shaped head with green icing and add the royal icing eyes while the green icing is still wet. Allow to dry for several hours Outline and flood the rim of the turtle shell with the tan icing. Draw a smile with a black food-colour pen and allow to dry completely.

Polar Bear with Skates

If there is one thing kids love more than cute animals, it is cute animals doing funny things – like a polar bear skating. Perfect for any winter occasion, or simply to raise a smile on a cold and frosty day.

SUPPLIES

- ♦ Polar bear cookie cutter
- ♦ Piping bag and nozzle
- ♦ White royal icing
- ♦ Black edible pearl
- ♦ Black food-colour pen
- ♦ Red food-colour pen
- ♦ Blue food-colour pen
- ♦ Pink food-colour pen
- ♦ Grey royal icing

1. Choose a basic cookie recipe on pages 7–8, and make a batch of cookies using a polar bear cutter. Allow the cookies to cool completely before decorating.

2. Outline the bear with white icing.

3. Flood the body and left leg with white icing and add a black pearl for the eye. Allow dry for about 20 minutes.

4. Flood the arm and right leg with white royal icing and allow to dry completely.

5. Draw a scarf with the black food-colour pen. Draw red and blue stripes onto the scarf.

6. Outline the body with the black food-colour pen and draw on ears, a nose, a mouth, arms and fingers.

7. Colour the inside of one ear and the cheek with pink marker.

8. Pipe a skate on each foot using grey icing and allow to dry completely.

TIPS & TRICKS

When I began decorating cookies, I got requests from friends to come up with something for their kids to decorate that was not too messy. Food-colour pens are the answer – they turn cookies into edible colouring books.

Mr & Mrs Polar Bear

Once I had designed the Mr & Mrs Bear cookies on page 67, I knew I had to make a polar bear version, too. Add sprinkles or sanding sugar, or use different coloured icing to customise. You can also follow the instructions to make panda bears – just add black icing.

SUPPLIES

- ◆ Bear face cookie cutter
- ◆ Piping bag and nozzle
- ◆ White royal icing
- ◆ Black edible pearls
- ◆ 1 small triangular and 1 medium oval noses (see page 16)
- ◆ Food safe paintbrush
- ◆ Pink food colour dust
- ◆ Black food-colour pen
- ◆ Edible flower decoration

1. Choose a basic cookie recipe on pages 7–8, and make a batch of cookies using a bear face cutter. Allow the cookies to cool completely before decorating.

2. Outline and flood the top of the face with white icing and add the black pearl eyes while the icing is still wet. Allow to dry for 20 minutes.

3. Flood the mouth area with white icing and add the royal icing nose while the icing is still wet. Allow to dry overnight.

4. Rub the food colour dust in a circle for the ears and cheeks using the paintbrush. Gently blow off the excess.

5. Draw the mouth with a black food-colour pen.

6. Add a dot of royal icing to the back of the edible flower and place it in Mrs Polar Bear's hair. Allow to dry for several hours.

Pelican

To make the pelican base cookies, cut a batch of flip-flop cookies and double the number of jellyfish cookies from your favourite basic cookie recipe (see pages 7–8). Before baking, use the bend of the flip-flop cutter to trim the legs from the jellyfish, so the legs will fit on the side of the flip-flops and resemble bird wings. Place the flip-flop cookie narrow end up and attach a jellyfish leg on either side. See page 12 for more on combining cookie cutters.

SUPPLIES

- ♦ Jellyfish cookie cutter
- ♦ Flip-flop cookie cutter
- ♦ Piping bag and nozzle
- ♦ Brown royal icing mixed with a touch of grey royal icing
- ♦ White royal icing
- ♦ Cocktail stick
- ♦ Orange royal icing
- ♦ Royal icing eyes (see page 15)
- ♦ Yellow royal icing beak (see page 17)
- ♦ Brown food-colour pen

1

Working quickly, outline and flood the outer half of 1 wing with brown icing. Outline and flood the inner half with white icing. While the icing is still wet, use a cocktail stick to feather the icing colours together. Repeat on the other wing and allow to dry for about 20 minutes.

2

Outline the body with a wavy line of white icing.

3

Flood the body with white icing. Pipe the legs and feet with orange icing.

4

Add the royal icing eyes and beak while the icing is still wet. Allow to dry completely. Draw a mouth with a brown food-colour pen.

Puffin

A really great thing about animal cookies is that you can make the same basic shape into very different finished cookies. This puffin uses the same base cookie shape as the Pelican on pages 100–101.

SUPPLIES

- Jellyfish cookie cutter
- Flip-flop cookie cutter
- Piping bag and nozzle
- White royal icing
- Black royal icing
- Small royal icing eyes (see page 15)
- Orange royal icing
- Royal icing beak (see page 17)

1. Choose a basic cookie recipe on pages 7–8, cut a batch of flip-flop cookies, and double the number of jellyfish cookies. Before baking, use the bend of the flip-flop cutter to trim the legs from the jellyfish, so the legs will fit on the side of the flip-flops and resemble bird wings. Place the flip-flop cookie narrow end up and attach a jellyfish leg on each side.

2. Outline the tummy and face with white icing and the body and wings with black icing.

3. Flood the tummy with white icing and add the royal icing eyes. Allow to dry completely.

4. Flood the wings and body with black icing.

5. Pipe the legs and feet with orange icing and allow to dry completely.

6. Place a dot of white icing onto the back of the royal icing beak. Place it under the eyes and gently press down.

Seagull

No ocean scene is complete without seagulls swooping from the sky. The seagull cookie uses the same basic techniques as the Pelican on pages 100–101.

SUPPLIES

- Jellyfish cookie cutter
- Flip-flop cookie cutter
- Piping bag and nozzle
- Grey royal icing
- White royal icing
- Black edible pearls
- Yellow royal icing beak (see page 17)
- Cocktail stick
- Orange royal icing

1. Choose a basic cookie recipe on pages 7–8, cut a batch of flip-flop cookies, and double the number of jellyfish cookies. Before baking, use the bend of the flip-flop cutter to trim the legs from the jellyfish, so the legs will fit on the side of the flip-flops and resemble bird wings. Place the flip-flop cookie narrow end up and attach a jellyfish leg on each side.

2. Outline the wings with grey icing and the body with white icing. Pipe the hair with white icing.

3. Flood the body with white icing and add the edible pearl eyes and the royal icing beak while the icing is wet.

4. Working quickly, flood the outer half of one wing with grey icing and the inner half with white icing. While the icing is still wet, use a cocktail stick to feather the icing colours together. Repeat on the other wing and allow to dry for 20 minutes.

5. Pipe the legs and feet using orange icing and allow to dry completely.

Yellow Penguin

I love all animals but, for some reason, I like penguins the most. The base cookie for this penguin combines cookie cutters, but it really could not be easier – cut a batch of hat cookies and an equal number of large circles using your favourite basic cookie recipe from pages 7–8. Before baking, simply press the hats firmly against the circles.

SUPPLIES

- ◆ Hat cookie cutter
- ◆ Large circle cookie cutter
- ◆ Piping bag and nozzle
- ◆ Black edible pearls
- ◆ Royal icing beak (see page 17)
- ◆ Yellow royal icing
- ◆ White royal icing
- ◆ White sanding sugar

1. Choose a basic cookie recipe on pages 7–8, and cut a batch of cookies using a hat and a large circle cutter. Before baking, trim the bottom of the hat cookie with the circle cookie cutter. Place the hat firmly against the circle.

2. Outline and flood the tummy and face with white icing. Add the black edible pearl eyes and the royal icing beak while the icing is still wet. Allow to dry completely.

3. Outline and flood the centre of the hat with yellow icing. Allow to dry completely.

4. Outline and flood the body with yellow icing and allow to dry for a few hours.

5. Outline and flood the trim and ball on the hat with white icing and sprinkle with sanding sugar while the icing is still wet. Shake off the excess sprinkles and allow to dry completely.

TIPS & TRICKS

It is fun to make a whole platter of these penguins in different colours, with contrasting hat and body colours. They work particularly well if you use two shades of the same colour, such as dark blue icing for the hat and a light blue for the body.

Polar Bears with Fish

These bears are made using an ice cream sundae cookie cutter. Cut the base cookies from a chosen cookie dough (see pages 7–8) and trim off the bottom of the sundae using a sharp knife before baking. To turn cookie decorating into a fun game for children, decorate the cookies to the end of step 3 and then let your little ones get creative with food-colour pens.

SUPPLIES

- ♦ Ice cream sundae cookie cutter
- ♦ Piping bag and nozzle
- ♦ White royal icing
- ♦ Black edible pearls
- ♦ Black food-colour pen
- ♦ Red food-colour pen

1

Outline the body with a wiggly line using white icing. Pipe the hat with white icing. Allow to dry for 20 minutes.

2

Flood the bear with white icing.

3

Add the pearl eyes while the icing is still wet and allow to dry for 20 minutes. Pipe a wonky circle using white icing and add a black pearl for the nose. Allow to dry completely.

4

Outline the scarf with a black food-colour pen and draw stripes with red and black food-colour pens. Draw a stripe onto the hat with a red food-colour pen.

5

Fill in any gaps on the scarf with a red food-colour pen. Outline the body, feet, arm and fish with a black food-colour pen. Draw two lines for eyebrows.

Lobster

The idea for this cookie came from a seafood restaurant when I was on holiday. The menu had a picture of a lobster alongside the description of the dish. I doodled on my napkin during dinner and made a cookie version. Look for ideas everywhere, you will be surprised what inspires you.

SUPPLIES

- ◆ Lobster cookie cutter
- ◆ Piping bag and nozzle
- ◆ White royal icing
- ◆ Small royal icing eyes (see page 15)
- ◆ Red royal icing
- ◆ Red sanding sugar
- ◆ Pink royal icing
- ◆ Black food-colour pen

1. Choose a basic cookie recipe on pages 7–8, and make a batch of cookies using a lobster cutter. Allow the cookies to cool completely before decorating.

2. Outline the body with white icing, piping in sections as photographed.

3. Flood the first and third body sections with white icing. While the icing is still wet, add the royal eyes and allow to dry completely.

4. Flood the second and fourth body sections with white icing and allow to dry completely.

5. Outline and flood the outer body and the outer claw with red icing. While the red icing is still wet, sprinkle with red sanding sugar and shake off the excess. Allow to dry for 20 minutes.

6. Outline and flood the inner claw with red icing and sprinkle with red sanding sugar while the icing is still wet. Shake off the excess.

7. Pipe 2 small pink dots for the cheeks.

8. Draw a mouth and eyebrows with a black food-colour pen. Allow to dry completely.

A Shoal of Puffer Fish

To make the puffer fish base cookie, you will need a large circle cookie cutter and a fish cutter. Cut a fish cookie from your chosen cookie dough (see page 7–8) and use the circle cutter to trim the fish cookie, allowing the top fin to act as eyes. Place the fish closely and firmly to the circle before baking. (For more tips on combining cookie cutters, see techniques on page 12.)

SUPPLIES

- ♦ Fish cutter
- ♦ Large circle cutter
- ♦ White royal icing
- ♦ Piping bag and nozzle
- ♦ Light pink royal icing
- ♦ Black edible pearls
- ♦ Dark pink royal icing
- ♦ Black food-colour pen

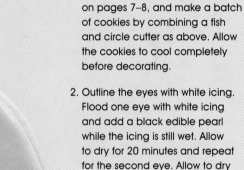

1. Choose a basic cookie recipe on pages 7–8, and make a batch of cookies by combining a fish and circle cutter as above. Allow the cookies to cool completely before decorating.

2. Outline the eyes with white icing. Flood one eye with white icing and add a black edible pearl while the icing is still wet. Allow to dry for 20 minutes and repeat for the second eye. Allow to dry completely.

3. Outline and flood the face with light pink icing. Allow to dry for 20 minutes.

4. Outline and flood the body with the dark pink icing. Allow to dry completely.

5. With a black food-colour pen, draw zigzag lines onto the top back and belly. Draw lines onto the tail and draw a mouth. Draw a fin with a half circle at the base and fill in the half circle.

Safari, Desert & Jungle Animals

Koala

Australia's most lovable tree huggers are always popular cookies. I have designed mine with a black nose because to me it is more koala-like, but their noses can be black or pink, so you can take your pick.

SUPPLIES

♦ Mouse face cookie cutter

♦ Piping bag and nozzle

♦ Dark grey royal icing

♦ Light grey royal icing

♦ Black edible pearls

♦ Black royal icing nose (see page 17)

♦ Pink food colour dust

♦ Food safe paintbrush

♦ Black food-colour pen

1. Choose a basic cookie recipe on pages 7–8, and make a batch of cookies using the mouse cutter. Allow the cookies to cool completely before decorating.

2. Outline and flood the inside of the ears with dark grey icing and allow to dry.

3. Outline and flood the outside of the ears and the head with light grey icing. While the icing is wet, add the black pearls for the eyes and the royal icing nose. Allow to dry completely.

4. Dip the dry tip of the paintbrush in the food colour dust and tap off the excess. Gently rub the cheeks in a circular motion and shake off the excess.

5. Draw a smile with the black food-colour pen.

TIPS & TRICKS

Animal cookie cutters can be used to create a surprising number of different animal cookies. A mouse cutter is not only used for this koala bear, it can also be used to make monkey, bear or ape cookies. And never feel you have to stick to the colours that nature gave animals.

Tiger

This brightly coloured tiger is made using the ever-versatile bus cookie cutter. Cut a batch of bus shapes from cookie dough and trim off the bumper before baking. Then simply turn the bus cookies upside down and presto, you have a tiger's face with the wheels as ears.

SUPPLIES

- ♦ Bus cookie cutter
- ♦ Piping bag and nozzle
- ♦ Orange royal icing
- ♦ Large royal icing eyes
- ♦ Large royal icing nose
- ♦ Black royal icing
- ♦ Black food-colour pen

1. Choose a basic cookie recipe on pages 7–8, and make a batch of cookies using the bus cutter. Trim the bumper before baking, and allow the cookies to cool completely before decorating.

2. Outline and flood the face with orange icing.

3. While the icing is still wet, add the royal icing eyes and the royal icing nose.

4. Using the wet-on-wet technique (see page 14), pipe stripes onto the cheeks and in between the ears using black icing. Allow to dry completely.

5. With a black food-colour pen, draw the ears and a short line down from the nose.

TIPS & TRICKS

Tigers are beautiful animals. They are fast, strong and graceful, not to mention the largest of all cat species. The next time you make tiger cookies, try making both orange and white tigers to mix things up.

Panda

To make the panda base cookie, cut a batch of large circles from a basic cookie recipe on pages 7–8, then cut twice the number of small circles. Trim the tops from the large circles and attach the smaller circles to either side of the head to make ears. (For more information on combining cookie cutters, see page 12.)

SUPPLIES
♦ Large circle cutter
♦ Small circle cutter
♦ Piping bag and nozzle
♦ White royal icing
♦ Black food-colour pen

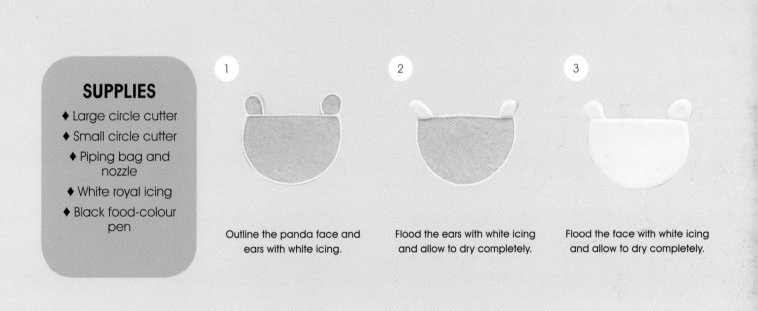

1
Outline the panda face and ears with white icing.

2
Flood the ears with white icing and allow to dry completely.

3
Flood the face with white icing and allow to dry completely.

4
Colour the eyes, ears and nose with a black food-colour pen, then draw a mouth.

5
Pipe two dots for the eyes with white icing.

Hippo

Who would have thought that a bus cookie cutter could be so versatile? To make the hippo base cookie, simply trim off the side view mirrors and bottom bumper (if your cutter has one) before baking the cookies. Turn the cookies upside down and magically, the wheels become teeth.

SUPPLIES

♦ Bus cookie cutter
♦ Piping bag and nozzle
♦ White royal icing
♦ Grey royal icing
♦ Large royal icing eyes (see page 15)
♦ Black royal icing
♦ Pink royal icing

1. Choose a basic cookie recipe on pages 7–8, and make a batch of cookies using the bus cutter, trimming off the side view mirrors and bottom bumper before baking. Allow the cookies to cool completely before decorating.

2. Outline and flood the teeth with white icing and allow to dry completely.

3. Outline and flood the face and ears with grey icing and add the royal icing eyes while the grey icing is still wet.

4. Pipe 2 black swirls for the nose.

5. Pipe the inside of the ears with pink icing and allow to dry completely.

TIPS & TRICKS

A front view bus cookie cutter (i.e., not one used to create a bus from a side angle) is available from all good cake and cookie suppliers (see page 144). It is incredibly versatile and perfect for creating quick and easy animal face cookies.

Zebra

Using a food-colour pen to decorate black and white cookies prevents the black icing from bleeding into the white.

Giraffe

No alterations are necessary to the bus base cookie here. Simply turn the 'bus' upside down and use the wheels for the ossicones (horns).

SUPPLIES

♦ Bus cookie cutter

♦ Piping bag and nozzle

♦ White royal icing

♦ Medium royal icing eyes (see page 15)

♦ Large triangular royal icing nose (see page 16)

♦ Black food-colour pen

1. Choose a basic cookie recipe on pages 7–8, and make a batch of cookies using the bus cutter, trimming off the bumper before baking. Allow the cookies to cool completely before decorating.

2. Outline and flood the zebra with white icing.

3. While the icing is still wet, add the royal icing eyes and royal icing nose and allow to dry completely.

4. Draw black stripes onto the cheeks and draw the mouth and hair with a black food-colour pen.

SUPPLIES

♦ Bus cookie cutter

♦ Ivory royal icing

♦ Brown royal icing

♦ Yellow royal icing

♦ Large royal icing eyes (see page 15)

♦ Pink royal icing

1. Choose a basic cookie recipe on pages 7–8, and make a batch of cookies using the bus cutter. Allow the cookies to cool completely before decorating.

2. Outline and flood the nose with ivory icing and pipe 2 dots for the nostrils using brown icing.

3. Outline and flood the top of the ossicones with brown icing.

4. Outline and flood the face and spiky hair with yellow icing. Using the wet-on-wet technique (see page 14), pipe brown spots onto the face.

5. While the icing is still wet, add the royal icing eyes.

6. Pipe the stem of the ossicones with brown icing.

7. Pipe the mouth with the ivory icing and, using the wet-on-wet technique (see page 14), pipe a pink line for the inside of the mouth. Allow to dry completely.

Lion

If you have an airbrush gun, try shading the edges of the lion's mane lightly with a warm brown airbrush colour. Hold the gun about 2.5cm (1in) from the cookie and gently spray around the edge of the mane. (For more advice on using an airbrush gun, see page 14.)

SUPPLIES

- ◆ Flower cookie cutter
- ◆ Piping bag and nozzle
- ◆ Reddish-brown royal icing
- ◆ Airbrush gun with brown airbrush colour (optional)
- ◆ Light brown royal icing
- ◆ Black edible pearls
- ◆ Black royal icing
- ◆ Black food-colour pen

1

Outline the edge of the cookie and the face with reddish-brown icing.

2

Flood the mane with reddish brown icing and allow to dry for a few hours.

3
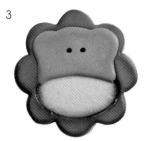
Outline and flood the face with the light brown icing and add 2 black edible pearls for the eyes while the icing is still wet. Allow to dry completely.

4

Flood the mouth with light brown icing and allow to dry completely. Pipe a triangle for the nose using black icing.

5

Draw a mouth, eyebrows, and dots to represent whiskers with a black food-colour pen.

A Herd of Elephants

Elephant cookies are very popular at baby showers and kids' birthday parties. Make a batch using different-sized cookie cutters to create an elephant family or a mother and her babies. Switch up the icing colours to suit the occasion.

SUPPLIES

- ♦ Elephant cookie cutter
- ♦ Piping bag and nozzle
- ♦ Blue-grey royal icing
- ♦ Black edible pearl

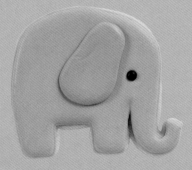

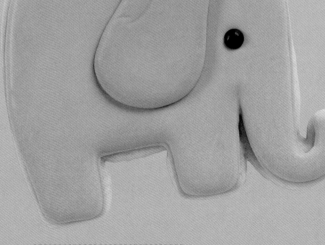

1. Choose a basic cookie recipe on pages 7–8, and make a batch of cookies using the elephant cutter. Allow the cookies to cool completely before decorating.

2. Outline and flood the elephant with blue-grey icing.

3. Add a black pearl for the eye, and allow to dry for 20 minutes.

4. Outline and flood the ear with blue-grey icing and allow to dry completely.

Camel

Did you know that a camel lives to be 40 or 50 years old? I bet these camel cookies will not last that long! If your camel cookie cutter has more than one hump, simply repeat the brown decoration. Or if you are really feeling creative, design and pipe a brightly coloured rug to go on the camel's back.

SUPPLIES

♦ Camel cookie cutter
♦ Piping bag and nozzle
♦ Tan royal icing
♦ Brown royal icing
♦ Medium royal icing eye (see page 15)

1. Choose a basic cookie recipe on pages 7–8, and make a batch of cookies using the camel cookie cutter. Allow the cookies to cool completely before decorating.

2. Outline the camel with a zigzag line using tan icing. Flood the camel with tan icing and add the royal icing eye while the icing is still wet.

3. Outline and flood the hump using brown icing and allow to dry completely.

A Barrel of Monkeys

Monkey cookies are just as popular as the monkey exhibit at the zoo! You do not need a special cutter to make a monkey cookie – just two different sized circle cutters. Cut a batch of large circles and double the number of medium circles from your favourite cookie dough (see page 7–8). Before baking, use the large circle cutter to cut notches out of the medium circle cookies, and place the medium circles firmly against the larger circles for the ears.

SUPPLIES

♦ Large circle cookie cutter

♦ Medium circle cutter

♦ Piping bag and nozzle

♦ Brown royal icing

♦ Tan royal icing

♦ Large royal icing eyes (see page 15)

♦ Royal icing nose (see page 16)

♦ Black or brown food-colour pen

1

Outline the monkey ears and head with brown icing. Outline the inside of the face and ears with tan icing.

2

Flood the inside of the face and inside of the ears with tan icing. Allow to dry completely.

3

Flood the outside of the ears and the head with brown icing.

4

While the icing is still wet, add the royal icing eyes allow to dry completely. Then add a dot of icing to the back of the nose and place it on the monkey's face. Allow to dry for several hours.

5

Draw eyebrows and a mouth with a black or brown food-colour pen.

Ostrich

The ostrich cookie is created using an acorn cookie cutter for the head, combined with an upside down rabbit (minus its ears) for the body.

SUPPLIES

- ◆ Acorn cookie cutter
- ◆ Rabbit with ears cookie cutter
- ◆ Piping bag and nozzle
- ◆ Light grey royal icing
- ◆ Large royal icing eyes (see page 15)
- ◆ Yellow royal icing
- ◆ Dark grey royal icing
- ◆ Black food-colour pen

1. Choose a basic cookie recipe on pages 7–8, and cut a batch of cookies using the acorn cutter and an equal number of cookies using the rabbit cutter. Before baking, trim the ears off the rabbit and use the bottom of the acorn cutter to cut a notch from the top of the rabbit cookies. Place the acorn cookie in the notch and bake. Allow the cookies to cool completely before decorating.

2. Outline and flood the face, neck and feet with the light grey icing. Add the royal icing eyes while the icing is still wet and allow to dry completely.

3. Outline and flood the beak with yellow icing.

4. Outline and flood the body of the ostrich with dark grey icing and allow to dry completely.

5. With a black food-colour pen, draw the mouth, eyelashes, nostrils, wings and the lines on the feet.

Colourful Bird

This cute bird cookie is made oh-so-simply using an egg cutter. To add extra detail, draw on a cute hat and scarf with food-colour pens.

SUPPLIES

- ◆ Egg cookie cutter
- ◆ Piping bag and nozzle
- ◆ Teal royal icing
- ◆ Royal icing beak (see page 17)
- ◆ Large royal icing eyes (see page 15)
- ◆ Orange royal icing

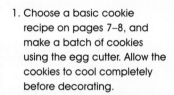

1. Choose a basic cookie recipe on pages 7–8, and make a batch of cookies using the egg cutter. Allow the cookies to cool completely before decorating.

2. Outline the bird and the wings with teal icing and allow to dry for 20 minutes.

3. Flood the bird with teal icing – be careful not to cover the lines of the wings.

4. While the icing is still wet, add the royal icing eyes and the royal icing beak.

5. Pipe the outer toes with orange icing. Allow to dry for about 10 minutes, then pipe the centre toes. Allow to dry completely.

Flamingo

The base cookie for this elegant flamingo is made by using heart and gift tag cookie cutters. Cut a batch of each from your chosen cookie dough, and use the heart cutter to trim the tag cookie so it will fit tightly to the side of the heart.

SUPPLIES

- ♦ Heart cookie cutter
- ♦ Tag cookie cutter
- ♦ Piping bag and nozzle
- ♦ Pink royal icing
- ♦ Medium royal icing eye (see page 15)
- ♦ Orange royal icing
- ♦ Black food colour gel
- ♦ Food safe paintbrush

1. Choose a basic cookie recipe on pages 7–8, and cut a batch of cookies using the heart and gift tag. Before baking, use the heart cutter to trim the tag so it will fit tightly to the side of the heart. Allow the cookies to cool completely before decorating.

2. Outline the flamingo body, neck and feathers with pink icing and allow to dry for 20 minutes.

3. Flood the body with pink icing – be careful not to cover the lines of the wings.

4. While the icing is still wet, add the royal icing eye and allow to dry completely.

5. Pipe the legs, feet and beak with orange icing and allow to dry for at least an hour.

6. Carefully paint the tip of the beak with black food colour gel mixed with water.

Toucan

The base cookie for the toucan is made by using a bird cutter and a rabbit with ears cutter. Cut a rabbit ear and a bird from your favourite cookie dough (see pages 7–8). Before baking, cut the end off the rabbit ear using the beak of the bird cutter. Attach the ear to the bird beak to form the toucan's large beak. (For more on combining cookie cutters, see page 12.)

SUPPLIES

- ♦ Bird cookie cutter
- ♦ Rabbit with ears cookie cutter
- ♦ Piping bag and nozzle
- ♦ White royal icing
- ♦ Black edible pearl
- ♦ Black royal icing
- ♦ Orange royal icing

1

Outline and flood a white oval for the eye and add a black pearl while the icing is still wet.

2

Outline the tail with black icing, including a central line.

3

Flood the tail with black icing. Outline and flood the beak with orange icing and allow the cookie to dry completely.

4

Outline the body and wing with the black icing and allow to dry for 20 minutes. Flood the body with the black icing and allow to dry completely.

A Puddle of Platypus

Did you know that the platypus is venomous? This mammal lays eggs, has a duck's bill, a beaver's tail and an otter's feet. Why does it need to be venomous? No one in their right mind would mess with such a strange creature! But it does make a cute cookie. Use an alligator cookie cutter and before baking the cookie, trim off the tip of the tail with a sharp knife.

SUPPLIES

♦ Alligator cookie cutter

♦ Piping bag and nozzle

♦ Brown royal icing

♦ Dark grey royal icing

♦ Black food-colour pen

1. Choose a basic cookie recipe on pages 7–8, and make a batch of cookies using the alligator cutter. Before baking, trim the tail with a sharp knife. Allow the cookies to cool completely before decorating.

2. Outline and flood the body of the platypus with brown icing.

3. Outline and flood the bill and feet with the dark grey icing and allow to dry completely.

4. Use the black food-colour pen to draw a few lines for the nose and 2 circles for the eyes.

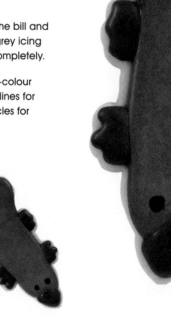

Crocodile

This cute croc may look like he is a completely different shape to the Platypus cookie on the opposite page, but both cookies are made using the same cookie cutter. The only adjustment I made to the base cookie shape was to cut the back right leg off before baking. The front right leg then becomes the eyes.

SUPPLIES

- Alligator cookie cutter
- Piping bag and nozzle
- White royal icing
- Black edible pearls
- Green royal icing

1. Choose a basic cookie recipe on pages 7–8, and make a batch of cookies using the alligator cutter. Before baking, cut off the back right leg with a sharp knife. Allow the cookies to cool completely before decorating.

2. Pipe a circle for the first eye with white icing and add a black pearl to the centre. Allow to dry for about 20 minutes.

3. Pipe the second eye and add a black pearl. Allow to dry completely.

4. Outline and flood the croc with green icing and allow to dry completely.

A Slither of Snakes

I live in the mountains of Tennessee, where rattlesnakes sometimes appear in my driveway and backyard. I am always amazed at how pretty the patterns on their backs are. I do not usually stick around long because the sound of the shaking tail can be a little frightening!

SUPPLIES

♦ Snake cookie cutter
♦ Piping bag and nozzle
♦ Tan royal icing
♦ Royal icing eye (see page 15)
♦ Brown royal icing
♦ Red royal icing

1. Choose a basic cookie recipe on pages 7–8, and make the batch of cookies using the snake cutter. Allow the cookies to cool completely before decorating.

2. Outline and flood the snake with the tan icing and add the royal icing while the icing is wet.

3. Pipe some zigzag lines with brown icing along the back.

4. Pipe a dot on the tip of the tail with brown icing.

5. Skip a space and pipe another dot with brown icing and allow to dry for about 20 minutes.

6. Pipe more brown icing dots for rattles in the spaces you skipped.

7. Pipe a red forked tongue and allow to dry completely.

Snake in a Jar

When I was a kid I spent hours in the yard catching butterflies, fireflies and frogs. My brother spent his time catching fish, frogs and (non-poisonous!) snakes. We would carefully place the creatures we caught into a glass jar so we could admire them, before setting them free. I loved looking at snakes in our jars and watching their tongues wiggle.

SUPPLIES

- ♦ Jar cookie cutter
- ♦ Piping bag and nozzle
- ♦ Grey royal icing
- ♦ White royal icing
- ♦ Brown food-colour pen
- ♦ Red food-colour pen
- ♦ Black food-colour pen
- ♦ Yellow food-colour pen
- ♦ Small royal icing eyes (see page 15)

1. Choose a basic cookie recipe on pages 7–8, and make a batch of cookies using the jar cutter. Allow the cookies to cool completely before decorating.

2. Outline the jar and lid with grey icing.

3. Flood the top of the jar lid with grey icing and flood the jar with white icing. Allow to dry for 20 minutes.

4. Flood the bottom of the lid with grey icing.

5. Draw an outline of the snake in the jar with a brown food-colour pen. Add some brown zigzag lines on the back of the snake, and some rattles on the tail. Colour in the snake using the yellow food-colour pen.

6. Draw and colour the tongue with the red food-colour pen and outline it with the black food-colour pen.

7. Glue the royal icing eyes to the head using a drop of white icing on the back of each one.

TIPS & TRICKS

A great party activity is to give out iced cookies and food-colour pens to kids and let their imaginations run wild.

Prehistoric Animals

Dinosaur Eggs

Dinosaur eggs are fun to make and fill up a plate of dinosaur cookies wonderfully well. These eggs are made by breaking the icing once the top layer has crusted over. Choose a cookie recipe from pages 7–8 to make the base cookies, then get creative.

SUPPLIES

- ◆ Egg cookie cutter
- ◆ Piping bag and nozzle
- ◆ Royal icing in various colours
- ◆ Brown royal icing, mixed with a little water
- ◆ Cream royal icing, mixed with a little water
- ◆ Stiff food safe paintbrush

1

Outline the eggs with your chosen icing colour.

2

Flood the eggs with your chosen icing colour.

3

Dip the paintbrush in the watered down cream icing. Flick the thin icing onto the cookies to make spots. Repeat with the thinned brown icing. Allow to dry for a few hours, until the icing has formed a crust on top. Use your fingers to gently press down on the icing to make cracks. Allow to dry completely.

Stegosaurus

This stegosaurus cookie is decorated without sections. However, if you prefer, you could make the head, hood, body and horns stand out by outlining and flooding each separately. If you cannot find the exact shade of rusty red icing, mix together terracotta, red and brown food colour gels until the desired colour is achieved.

SUPPLIES

♦ Stegosaurus cookie cutter
♦ Piping bag and nozzle
♦ Green royal icing
♦ Black edible pearl
♦ Rusty red royal icing

1. Choose a basic cookie recipe on pages 7–8 and make a batch of cookies using a stegosaurus cookie cutter. Allow the cookies to cool completely before decorating.

2. Outline and flood the body with green icing. While the icing is still wet, add a black pearl eye. Allow to dry for several hours.

3. Outline and flood the spikes with rusty red icing. Allow to dry completely.

TIPS & TRICKS

The great thing about creating dinosaur cookies is that nobody really knows what they are supposed to look like! If you go online, you will find pictures of Stegosaurus in many different colours and patterns. Take a look and see which colour combination you like best.

Pterodactyl

I have kept this cookie nice and easy by simply flooding the body, head and wings with one colour icing. However, if you would like to give your cookie more detail, you could pipe the beak in a different colour or make the wings more defined by outlining and piping them in sections.

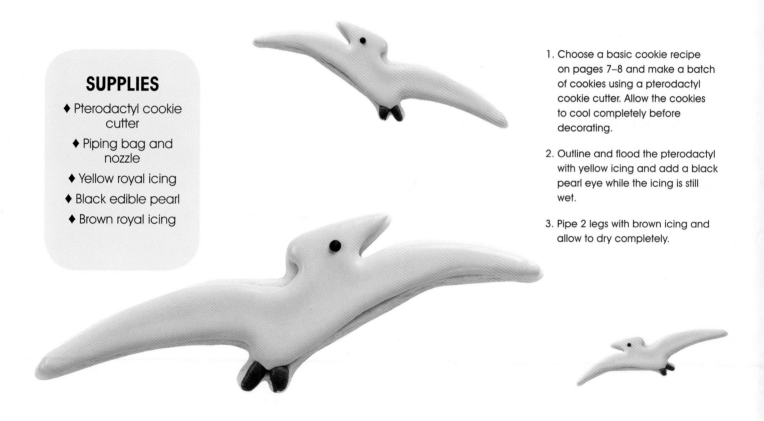

SUPPLIES

♦ Pterodactyl cookie cutter
♦ Piping bag and nozzle
♦ Yellow royal icing
♦ Black edible pearl
♦ Brown royal icing

1. Choose a basic cookie recipe on pages 7–8 and make a batch of cookies using a pterodactyl cookie cutter. Allow the cookies to cool completely before decorating.

2. Outline and flood the pterodactyl with yellow icing and add a black pearl eye while the icing is still wet.

3. Pipe 2 legs with brown icing and allow to dry completely.

TIPS & TRICKS

Why not make prehistoric animal cookies for a kid's party? Once the cookies are baked, let the kids ice them and add their own details using sprinkles or food-colour pens.

T-Rex

T-Rex dinosaurs are very recognisable with their big heads and small arms. I have designed this cookie with yellow spots, but you can pipe the spots in any colour you want. Use a cocktail stick or skewer to add texture to the icing as it dries to create scales or rough skin. Choose a cookie recipe from pages 7–8 to make the base cookies.

SUPPLIES

♦ T-Rex cookie cutter

♦ Piping bag and nozzle

♦ Green royal icing

♦ Small royal icing eye (see page 15)

♦ Yellow royal icing

1

Outline the T-Rex, including the lines for the legs and arms, with green icing.

2

Wait a few minutes so the outlines of the arm and legs will show, then flood with green icing. Add a royal icing eye while the green icing is still wet.

3

Pipe a few spots of various sizes onto the T-Rex's back with yellow icing. Allow to dry completely.

Triceratops

Dinosaur cookies are a real crowd pleaser and make a great gift. Kids will love handing these out to their friends and teachers and dazzling them with their dinosaur knowledge.

Velociraptor

This dinosaur found fame in the film *Jurassic Park*. Although a vicious and deadly predator, it is easy to make it look a bit less scary in cookie form!

SUPPLIES

- ◆ Triceratops cookie cutter
- ◆ Piping bag and nozzle
- ◆ Dark blue royal icing
- ◆ Light blue royal icing
- ◆ Black edible pearl

1. Choose a basic cookie recipe on pages 7–8 and make a batch of cookies using a triceratops cookie cutter. Allow the cookies to cool completely before decorating.

2. Outline the triceratops with dark blue icing.

3. Flood with light blue icing and add a black pearl eye while the icing is still wet.

4. Pipe the horns with dark blue icing and allow to dry completely.

SUPPLIES

- ◆ Velociraptor cookie cutter
- ◆ Piping bag and nozzle
- ◆ Orange royal icing
- ◆ Small royal icing eye (see page 15)
- ◆ Black royal icing

1. Choose a basic cookie recipe on pages 7–8 and make a batch of cookies using a velociraptor cookie cutter. Allow the cookies to cool completely before decorating.

2. Outline and flood the velociraptor with orange icing.

3. While the icing is still wet, add a royal icing eye and pipe black lines along the neck and down the back. Allow to dry completely.

Parasaurolophus

To make a prehistoric-themed centrepiece for a party, bake three round sponge cakes of different sizes. Stack them on top of each other and decorate to look like a volcano, then place Parasaurolophus cookies all around the volcano.

SUPPLIES

♦ T-Rex cookie cutter
♦ Letter 'T' cookie cutter
♦ Piping bag and nozzle
♦ Yellow royal icing
♦ Orange royal icing
♦ Royal icing eye (see page 15)

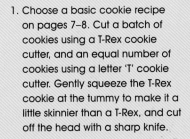

1. Choose a basic cookie recipe on pages 7–8. Cut a batch of cookies using a T-Rex cookie cutter, and an equal number of cookies using a letter 'T' cookie cutter. Gently squeeze the T-Rex cookie at the tummy to make it a little skinnier than a T-Rex, and cut off the head with a sharp knife.

2. Trim off about 1cm (½in) from the bottom of the 'T' cookie and place the 'T' cookie snugly against the top of the T-Rex body to form the Parasaurolophus's head. (For tips on combining cookie cutters, see page 12.) Bake, and allow the cookies to cool completely before decorating.

3. Outline and flood the Parasaurolophus with yellow icing and add a royal icing eye while the icing is still wet.

4. Pipe triangles onto the back and a long triangle onto the head with orange icing. Allow to dry completely.

Woolly Mammoth

I tried to make a woolly mammoth cookie from a butterfly cutter, but it was not working, so I called a friend to ask for advice. She suggested using a cupcake cutter, and it worked perfectly. I have been using a cupcake cutter for these cookies ever since. Choose a cookie recipe from pages 7–8 to make the base cookies.

SUPPLIES

- ♦ Cupcake cookie cutter
- ♦ Piping bag and nozzle
- ♦ Reddish brown royal icing
- ♦ Large royal icing eyes (see page 15)
- ♦ White royal icing
- ♦ Large royal icing teeth (see page 17)
- ♦ Dark brown royal icing

1

Outline the woolly mammoth with a zigzag line with reddish brown icing. Pipe the lines for the ears and legs.

2

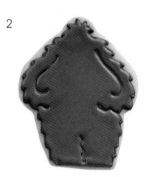

Flood the mammoth with reddish brown icing – be careful not to cover the lines for the ears and legs.

3

Add the royal icing eyes while the reddish brown icing is still wet. Allow to dry for 20 minutes. Pipe the toes with white icing.

4

Outline the trunk with reddish brown icing.

5

Flood the trunk in sections. Glue the royal icing teeth in place using a little white royal icing. Pipe the hair with dark brown icing and allow to dry completely.

Sabre-toothed Tiger

The base cookie for my sabre-toothed tiger is made using my beloved bus cookie cutter. These cookies are easy to make and the kids can have fun placing the eyes, teeth and nose on the face when the icing is still wet.

SUPPLIES

♦ Bus cookie cutter

♦ Piping bag and nozzle

♦ Yellow royal icing

♦ Royal icing teeth (see page 17)

♦ Large royal icing eyes (see page 15)

♦ Large royal icing nose (see page 16)

1. Choose a basic cookie recipe on pages 7–8 and make a batch of cookies using a bus cookie cutter. Trim off the bumper before baking and allow the cookies to cool completely before decorating.

2. Turn the bus cookie upside-down, so the wheels become ears.

3. Outline the tiger with yellow icing, including the mouth section.

4. Flood the mouth with yellow icing and add the royal icing teeth while the yellow icing is still wet. Allow to dry for 20 minutes.

5. Flood the face and ears. While the icing is still wet, add the royal icing nose and eyes. Allow to dry completely.

TIPS & TRICKS

You can totally change the look of your Sabre-toothed Tiger by adding some shading with an airbrush, or by drawing whiskers with a brown or black food-colour pen.

Green and Red Diplodocus

Long neck dinosaur cookie cutters are probably the easiest of all cutters to find. They come in many sizes and the finished cookies look great decorated in multiple colours. To make these two Diplodocus cookies I have used two slightly different shaped cutters from different suppliers – see what you can find and experiment with different shapes.

SUPPLIES

- ♦ Long neck dino cookie cutter
- ♦ Piping bag and nozzle
- ♦ Green royal icing
- ♦ Brown royal icing
- ♦ Black edible pearl

1. Choose a basic cookie recipe on pages 7–8 and make a batch of cookies using a long neck dino cookie cutter. Allow the cookies to cool completely before decorating.

2. Outline and flood the diplodocus with green icing.

3. While the icing is still wet, add a black pearl for the eye. Pipe spots onto the back with brown icing and allow to dry completely.

SUPPLIES

- ♦ Long neck dino cookie cutter
- ♦ Piping bag and nozzle
- ♦ Rusty red royal icing
- ♦ Turquoise royal icing
- ♦ Small royal icing eye (see page 15)

1. Chose a basic cookie recipe on pages 7–8 and make a batch of cookies using a long neck dino cookie cutter. Allow the cookies to cool completely before decorating.

2. Outline and flood the diplodocus with rusty red icing (see the introduction on page 134 for tips on making this colour icing).

3. While the icing is still wet, add the royal icing eye. Pipe spots onto the back with turquoise icing and allow to dry completely.

TIPS & TRICKS

Dinosaur cookies are loved by boys and girls. It is easy to plan a birthday or cookie decorating party with dinosaur cookies because they can be decorated with any colour, sprinkles or sweets.

Index

Suppliers

Ann Clark cutters available from
www.foosecookiecutters.com
www.karenscookies.net

Cakes, Cookies and Crafts Shop
www.cakescookiesandcraftsshop.
co.uk

Cake Craft Shop
www.cakecraftshop.co.uk

Hobbycraft
www.hobbycraft.co.uk

John Lewis
www.johnlewis.com

Karen's Cookies
www.karenscookies.net

Lakeland
www.lakeland.co.uk

Legend Cookshops
www.legendcookshop.co.uk

Not on the High Street
www.notonthehighstreet.com

Squires Kitchen
www.squires-shop.com

The Sugar Shack
www.sugarshack.com

Wilton
www.wilton.com

Windsor Craft Limited
www.windsorcakecraft.co.uk